To Tony & Cindy
Enjoy the book
and St. Louis
history

Jerry

Journeys:

The Gamaches in the New World

Marquis de Gamache

JOURNEYS: THE GAMACHES IN THE NEW WORLD

BY

MARQUIS DE GAMACHE

AuthorHouse™
1663 Liberty Drive, Suite 200
Bloomington, IN 47403
www.authorhouse.com
Phone: 1-800-839-8640

© 2008 Marquis de Gamache. All rights reserved.

No part of this book may be reproduced, stored in a retrieval system, or transmitted by any means without the written permission of the author.

First published by AuthorHouse 3/12/2008

ISBN: 978-1-4343-4819-7 (sc)

Printed in the United States of America
Bloomington, Indiana

This book is printed on acid-free paper.

Preface

For almost 2000 years in Europe the Gamache family name has been in existence. We are related to William the Conquer, Queen Elizabeth II of Great Britain, and the singer Madonna. One of our ancestors, Hugues de Gamache went on the first Crusade in 1096 and his name and coat-of-arms hangs in the Hall of the Crusaders at the palace of Versailles.

This book is an historical chronology of the Gamache's voyage to the new world and their part in the establishment of two countries – Canada and the United States. Some of the research comes from the Internet, some from family stories, and still more from interviews with family members and a trip to Quebec to discuss joint research interests with Lisette Gamache who has researched the Gamache family for 30 years.

Gamache Family Archives

The author (l), Lisette Gamache, and Rynard Gamache

With over 10,000 Gamache's in the United States and Canada, with 500 still in France, this story has only touched one small part of family history.

A word of caution is advised. Similar to historical or genealogical research that is multi-dimensional, dates are often reported in error. For example, a birth date might be mistaken for a christening date or the date of death might be mistaken for the date of internment. Often, people judge by comparison with other known dates that may lead to inaccurate conclusions. I am sure that some dates reported are in error, there was an effort to ensure at least two or three references for a date existed before reporting it. There is also the possibility that individuals conducting the federal census every ten years may not have recorded facts appropriately. For example, our great grandmother was named "Madora" not "Eudora"; however, she was referred to as "Dora". Only two Eudora Gamache's were found, a 15 year-old servant girl reported on a census in St. Louis in the late nineteenth century and a woman who married in St. Louis in 1873.

This story starts in Normandy, where during the first century B.C., one of its first great invasions by the Romans occurred. The area became an important part of the Holy Roman Empire until the 4th century. In the 9th century, Vikings or Norsemen raided the land and gave it the name – Normandy.

Hrolf Rognvaldsson (c. 860 – c. 932), Earl of Orkney (Scotland), a title he inherited from his father Rognvald, was one of the lesser leaders of the Viking fleet that besieged Paris in 885 under Sigfred, leader of the Vikings. The Anglicized name of Hrolf is Rollo. In 886, when Sigfred retreated in return for tribute from the citizens of Paris, Rollo stayed behind and was sent to raid and sack Burgundy. Later, Rollo returned to the Seine region with his followers. He invaded the area of northern France now known as

Normandy. Unlike most Vikings whose intentions were to plunder Frankish lands, Rollo's true intentions were to look for lands to settle.

After many battles with the Vikings, the French King Charles the Simple, understood that he could no longer hold back their advances, and decided as a temporary measure to give Rollo land around Rouen with the condition that he would convert to Christianity and defend the Seine River from other raiding Vikings.

In the Treaty of Saint-Clair-sur-Epte in the year 911 with King Charles, Rollo pledged feudal allegiance to the king and converted to Christianity, probably with the baptismal name Robert of Normandy, since he had married Poppa, Duchess of Normandy, thus becoming the first Duke of Normandy. In return, and in admission of defeat, King Charles granted Robert the lower Seine area (today's upper Normandy) and the titular rule of Normandy, centered in the city of Rouen.

Gamache Family Archives

Rollo on the Six Dukes statue in the town of Falaise, France.

Gamache Family Archives

Statue of Rollo in Rouen

Robert stayed true to his word of defending the shores of the Seine in accordance to the Treaty of Saint-Clair-sur-Epte, but in time he and his followers had very different ideas. Robert began to divide the land between the Epte and Risle rivers among his chieftains and he, himself, settled there with a de facto capital in Rouen. With these settlements, Robert began to further raid other Frankish lands, now from the security of a settled homeland, rather than a mobile fleet. Eventually, however, Robert's men intermarried with the local women, and became more settled as Frenchmen. At the time of his death, Robert's expansion of his territory had extended as far west as the Vire River.

Gamache Family Archives

Rollo's grave at the cathedral of Rouen

Sometime around 927, Robert passed the fief in Normandy to his son, William Longsword. Robert may have lived for a few years after that, but certainly died before 933. Even though Robert (Rollo) had converted to Christianity, some of his pagan roots surfaced at the end. As Robert's death drew near, he had a hundred Christian prisoners beheaded in front of him to honor of the gods whom he had worshipped. Afterwards, in remorse, he distributed a hundred pounds of gold around to churches in honor of the true god in whose name he had accepted baptism.

Rollo is a direct ancestor of William the Conqueror. Through William, he is a direct ancestor and predecessor of the present-day British royal family, including Elizabeth II of the United Kingdom of Great Britain and Northern Ireland. Inger (Inczar), the brother of Rollo, founded the Gamache family in Normandy and England. Our ancestry can be traced back to Finland (Fornjotur, King of Kvenland c. 160 A.D.) by way of Sweden and Norway.

The Gamache's Normandy evolved into the royal dynasty of Plantagenet, in the 12th century, and England expanded its claims to continental land when Henry II of England, Duke of Normandy, married Eleanor of Aquitaine in 1152. Thomas de Saint Valèry de Gamache established the Gamache coat of arms which denotes a blue sky over a silver field.

Gamache Family Archives

Coat-of-Arms designed by Thomas de Saint Valery
about 1180

We know from genealogy and the National Geographic Research on genographic data (DNA) that Gamache family ancestors came from northern France (Normandy). However, there is uncertainty of what happened between Inczar Gamache's life and the late 1500's in France. At the end of the Dark Ages and throughout the Middle Ages, pieces of Gamache history have surfaced in archival records, church documents, and museums. Piecing together these data from the 9th Century to the 16th century is like putting together a historical and genealogical puzzle, with half the pieces missing. Eight hundred years of Gamache history is a mystery. Perhaps France's church records and dusty libraries shelves may hold the answer.

The failure of King Philippe Auguste of France to gain possession of Normandy from the English Plantagenet in the 1400's became one of the primary causes of the Hundred Years War. The people and landscape of Normandy suffered dearly from this long conflict. Normandy was, however, finally secured by France in 1450 and became a semi-autonomous state.

In the 15th century the Count de Gamache fought along side of Joan of Arc. Quite honestly, according to record, he did not think too highly of this peasant upstart.

There are a variety of explanations on the origin of the name Gamache. The Latin word for leg is "gama"; the same in Italian. The name would indicate something to do with legs. One explanation was the name Gamache were chaps or riding breeches that protected a rider's legs from dew or thrones while riding through the bramble-bush in the mornings in Normandy. Gamaches were made, either of leather or cloth and included a covering for shoes.

Gamache Family Archive

Checkered Gamaches

Another explanation is an area in Normandy, including towns, named Gamaches, which may resemble geographical legs.

Our story starts where data resumes in the year 1565 in Normandy, France, specifically in the Picard region. Queen Elizabeth I was on the throne in England and Shakespeare was a year old. Mary, Queen of Scots, ruled Scotland until she abdicated in 1567. Charles IX ruled France. Pedro Menendez de Aviles founded St. Augustine, Florida. The Pope was Gregory XIII, and Protestantism was growing in Europe following Martin Luther's lead in 1517. Michelangelo (1475 – 1564) was the leading artist of his time.

France, as well as most of Europe, was ruled by a feudal system much as it had been for centuries past. With the discovery of the new world, France laid claim to New France (Canada) that was established under the sponsorship of the French Kings and with the feudal system intact. Gamache ancestors arrived in New France in 1652, but their restless nature and dreams of land soon compelled them to volunteer as guides and trappers with French explorers who roamed the Ohio and Mississippi valley. Eventually, they came to the east coast of the Mississippi, explored the Mississippi and helped founded the city of St. Louis.

It seems a large part of military history escaped the family. There were a few notable exceptions. Gamaches fought in the Hundred Year War in France; the American Revolution; and the Civil War; although these last two examples did not involve any of the author's direct ancestors. It seems this direct line was singularly unconcerned with political and military matters. To a large part, this ambivalence can be traced to geographic location. The family was in Québec twenty years after the landing at Plymouth Rock, fifty years after Jamestown, and was settled in the St. Louis area before and during the Revolution. It was not pacifism that prevented military service – it was opportunity. What happened in the Revolution was of little interest to those in French North America. This was particularly true in the St. Louis area where the political landscape was changing between France and Spain long before the Louisiana Purchase that almost doubled the size of the United States. An interesting story – Jefferson Barracks and the War of 1812 are told in several pages in this book.

While this book combines genealogical history with that of known historical facts in the manner of other writers; it is not a listing of who begot whom. Rather, the effort is to make genealogy come alive with reference to historical events surrounding the Gamache forbearers. To this extent, the author has relied upon public knowledge, including consulting the Internet for certain histories that have been incorporated with this book. Where possible, if the source can be identified, appropriate recognition is given.

So many people have assisted in this writing. Jack Underwood from the Arnold Missouri Historical Society; Jefferson

College and the University of Missouri archivists; Nancy May, a distant relative contacted through the Internet; as well as many Internet sites including ancestory.com, familytree.com, and genealogy.com. All are appreciated for their help. I want to especially thank Marcel Catellier, the Maire (Mayor) of Cap St. Ignace for his hospitality and his dedicated staff.

Gamache Family Archives

Maire Marcel Catellier and the author

I dedicate this book to Jack Underwood, to my brother Rynard, who shares my interest in genealogy, to my sister Sharon, my children David, Kim, Erik, and Sarah, my granddaughter Jessica, my niece Marsha, and her children Blake and Kyle. All of whom are the real benefactors of this book – you have each been an inspiration to me.

I want to offer a special thank you to Dr. Mili Koger, my wife, and Rynard Gamache, my brother, for editing this work and to Mary Gamache, my sister-in-law and Gisele Alias of Lyon, France for their invaluable work in translating archived French documents. This has been a family project. To my sister Sharon, who was busy taking care of her mother-in-law, your e-mails have provided much needed encouragement and special thanks for accompanying me to St. Louis cemeteries to photograph gravestones.

GLG

St. Augustine, Florida
geraldgamache@bellsouth.net

A SALUTE TO THOSE THAT ORGANIZE FAMILY HISTORY

Each day I thank God, as I behold Him face to face
In hearts and minds of believers in the human race

That exercise their faith to learn and teach the facts
of our great heritage, like found in the Book of Acts

Our great heritage, discovered from families past
to note diligently each, etched in memory to last

To write down their discovery, notes so profound
noted in books well organized and so neatly bound

So that generations to come too will find their place
offering up thanks, as they behold God face to face

Our Creator the source of all we have here on earth
set in the spotlight of our work, judge of their worth

Thank you Lord for each, that search and organize
may they in the end accomplish Heaven's great prize

Jack Underwood
August 2007

Dedicated to Dr. Jerry Gamache's tireless effort to do exactly what these notes in rhyme suggest. May God richly bless the work of his heart, mind and hands. Jerry's ancestors here in America, include Jean Baptiste Gamache, a believer named after another who wandered in the wilderness announcing the coming of the Lord.

Journeys: The Gamache in the New World

Chapter 1

In the small town of Mantes-la-Jolie, which was settled on the western edge of Paris since before the 11th century, a new winter day was beginning. This village was burned to the ground in 1087 by William the Conqueror, bastard son of Robert, Duke of Normandy. In the battle to secure its capture, William, who was crowned King of England almost twenty years earlier in 1066, received a fatal injury and died on September 9. Now, in the year of Our Lord, fifteen hundred and sixty-five, a journey began at the church, which was seven miles away from the Gamache home. This journey would end 442 years later in St. Augustine, Florida, founded also in 1565 at another Gamache house – the author's.

On a spring day, it would be a pleasant journey, but now in the coldest cold of winter it was a step-by-step agony. Père Jacques adjusted his scarf that covered his nose and cheeks. Bent over against the wind he began reciting the Our Father to get his mind off the bitter cold. "Pater noster, qui es in caelis, sanctificetur nomen tuum. Adveniat regnum tuum, fiat voluntas tua, sicut in caelo, et in terra." Just then, the snow cleared for a moment; he could see in the distance, the roof of Gamache's home. Finally, after three hours of walking he was nearing his destination.

No one expected the Father to walk through a blinding snowstorm to baptize a newborn baby. But, they never knew Père Jacques. It was his duty. When he heard about the birth, he gathered his holy water and alba and dressed for the journey. Babies did not live long, especially in the wintertime; so baptism was essential to save a young soul. Besides, he reminded himself that at 49 years of age he hoped he would soon be called to heaven where he hoped that sacrifices like this would be pleasing to Our Lord.

The knock on the heavy door was accompanied by loud barking of a huge dog, one that had been interrupted from intently looking at the stirring of the pot hung over the smoldering wood in the fireplace. Once inside, Père Jacques' layers of clothes were removed, and the table close to the fire was cleared for the guest. There was warmth and the smell of rabbit stew, an aroma that filled the simple one room home. First things first – there was a need for a half hour of warmth sitting by the fire. Then the baby, **Guillaume Lamarre Gamache**, was presented to Père Jacques.

Author's Note: Bold print signifies the author's direct relationship to this person.

What a strong and healthy baby he was; the parents beamed with pride. The baptismal ceremony did not take long. Now one more soul was added to the Catholic faith. This was important as the new Protestant teachings were infecting the diocese. This had been a Catholic area of France for as long as anybody could imagine. Rouen, a short distant away to the South, was the location where a hundred years before Joan of Arc led her troops to make her stand against the English. But times had changed. Now the Catholic Church had competition for souls. Years ago, babies were baptized on the first anniversary of their birth, but not now. Père Jacques had to admit those were the thoughts running through his mind as he prepared to come to this baptism.

Before returning once again to the church, Père Jacques sat down with the parents to eat fresh rabbit stew and thick venison sausages, which covered the warm bread. Fully nourished for the long trip back; he was on the road back to town.

Years turned into decades, life in the small village stayed the same. The crosses in the cemetery next to the church had multiplied and included one for Père Jacques. New babies were born to replace those who had died. The year Guillaume (William) Lamarre Gamache was born turned; in time it was the end of the 16th century.

Chapter 2

As the 1500's gave way to the 1600's two important events happened in Gamache history. First, Guillaume Lamarre Gamache married **Renee Huan** around 1590. Second, their only son, **Nicolas Gamache** was born about 1595. Although he died in 1676 in France, Nicolas was to play a pivotal role in the founding of New France.

Nicolas married twice. He married his first wife, Michele Potel, around 1618. She died leaving one child Jacques. Jacques was born in 1626 at Breval, Yvelines, Normandy, (Guillaume' birth place). Jacques would die in New France in the year 1681, thus becoming the first Gamache buried in the new world.

After his wife died around 1628, Nicolas married **Jacqueline Cadotte**. She was born in 1601 and the marriage took place on July 9, 1629. The marriage to Jacqueline produced two children, Genevieve on October 13, 1636, and **Nicolas Lamarre**, born April 17, 1639 at St. Illiers-la-Ville, Chartres.

During the period from the late 1500's to the early 1700's several events dominated French life and influenced Gamache history. The spread of the Protestant Reformation, particularly the

Calvanists, threatened France's allegiance to Roman Catholicism. In the 16th century, John Calvin's teachings began to spread widely. Many nobles converted, some because they thought Calvin right, others because Calvinism was a convenient excuse for resisting the growing power of the Catholic kings of France.

These tensions led to French Wars of Religion (1562-1598). During this period, the Catholics battled the Calvinist Huguenots for control of the monarchy. The fact that France had two weak monarchs: Charles IX (r. 1560-74) and Henry III (r. 1574-89) allowed rival aristocratic factions to align along opposing religious lines. The minority Huguenots, led by Gaspard de Coligny and Louis de Conde, were supported from 1562 to 1576 by external Protestant armies in their conflict with the Catholic crown.

There was a lull in the fighting in 1572, and King Charles IX wanted to make peace. He arranged a marriage between his sister and Henri of Navarre, a leader of the Calvinists. The wedding was to be held in Paris on St. Bartholomew's Day. Catherine de Medici, the wife of Charles IX persuaded the king to kill all the Calvinist nobles who had journeyed to Paris for the wedding and were not prepared to offer much resistance. On the night of 24 August 1572 around 50,000 Huguenots were slaughtered in the Saint Bartholomew's Day massacre.

Word spread that it was acceptable to kill Calvinists, so people used the occasion to settle all sorts of private disputes. Debtors killed Calvinist creditors. Rejected suitors killed Calvinists who had turned them down. Students killed Calvinist teachers. After the massacre, the Politiques, a party of moderate Catholics, emerged under the family of Montmorency. In 1576 the Holy League, a Catholic extremist party led by the house of Guise, was formed for the purpose of opposing the peace with the Protestants accorded by King Henri III. However, after the death of Henri III the Bourbon, the Protestant leader Henri of Navarre became heir to the throne as Henri IV.

Henri of Navarre first converted to Catholicism to save his life, but then decided he was a Calvinist after all and led Calvinists to victory after victory on the battlefield. In 1589, he held all France except Paris and some historians say he had a hand in assassination of Henri III later that year. Whatever the case, Henri of Navarre became Henri IV, and his opponents continued to fight against him, even after his re-conversion to Catholicism in 1593 so Parisians would accept him as their king.

Henri IV worked hard at economic development and encouraged the fur trade between New France and France. He drained swamps in France for more cultivated land. He also was truly concerned with peasant welfare, promising "a chicken in every peasant's pot every Sunday." The king eventually defeated the Holy League, but in 1598 he issued the Edict of Nantes, which lasted until 1685, the edict that made France Catholic. There were no Calvinist churches near Paris, but the Edict allowed Calvinists to practice their religion openly elsewhere and gave the control of certain fortified cities to the Calvinists.

Henri IV was hated by extremist elements of both Catholics and Calvinists. He was assisinated by a Catholic extremist. Henri's carriage became stuck in traffic, and he stabbed him to death. Henri left as his heir a 9-year old son--Louis XIII

Louis XIII was timid, morose, and in poor health and his greatest accomplishment was siring Louis XIV, the Sun King. January 1636, Louis XIII chose Charles Hualt de Montmagny as the first governor of New France. The Jesuits sent written reports that were published annually as *Relations* in France. Superior Paul le Jeune wrote the *Relations* from 1632 to 1640, and these accounts encouraged others to support or participate in their endeavors. The 1636 *Relations* suggested how people of moderate means could find success in New France.

In the 1650s, Montreal still had only a few dozen settlers, and a severely under populated New France almost fell completely to the Iroquois attempts to drive out the French. In 1660, settler Adam Dollard des Ormeaux led a militia and Huron allies against a much larger Iroquois force. None of the militia survived, but they accomplished reversing the Iroquois invasion. In 1663, New France finally became more secure when Louis XIV made it a province of France. In 1665, he sent a French garrison, the Carignan-Salières regiment, to Québec. The government of the colony was reformed along the lines of the government of France, with the Governor General and Intendant subordinate to the Minister of the Marine in France. In 1665 Jean Talon was sent by the Minister of the Marine, Jean-Baptiste Colbert, to New France as the first Intendant (Administrator). These reforms limited the power of the Bishop of

Québec, who had held the greatest amount of power after the death of Champlain, December 25, 1635.

In the winter of 1665-1666, Jean Talon conducted the census of New France. It showed a population of 3,215 was more than there had been only a few decades earlier. But the census showed a great difference in the number of men (2034) and women (1181).

In the mid-seventeenth century, the French King Louis XIV sent almost 1,200 French officers to fight the Iroquois in New France. After the war, the soldiers were forced to remain in the colony. Many wanted to set up their own farms, but since young, unmarried women were scarce, few could afford to do so. Female as well as male labor was required for farming.

Between 1664 and 1672, the King, recognizing these problems, ordered nearly 800 young women sent to New France. Colorful stories and myths have grown up around this group of young French women, called *les filles du roi* (daughters of the King). Some legends describe them as illegitimate children, or daughters of prison inmates. In fact, these women came from varied social and geographical backgrounds. While almost half were from the Parisian orphanage, a third were from Western France (mainly

Normandy and Poitou.) Most were from the lower classes and about one-third of the poorest were provided with dowries by the crown.

Marguerite Bourgeois, who served as the "mother figure" to each of these young women, wrote that in about six weeks, all *les filles du roi* were married! By 1772, the population of southwest Montréal, where the young women settled, had already doubled!

Chapter 3

Back in Normandy, a long time friend of Nicolas, Père Renè was installed as a Jesuit priest in the Cathedral at Rouen. One spring day in 1651 as he was cleaning the sacristy he was surprised to see, through the window, his friend Nicolas Gamache dismounting his horse. Having ridden over a hundred miles, the visit must be important. When Nicolas was seated at a table he said, "I have been thinking of going to New France and taking the family with me. I value your advice. " "Geneviève is barely 17 and young Nicolas is 13! You can't be serious!" Renè replied. "There is nothing here for the children. No opportunities. Protestants are everywhere and intrigue fills the air. I want the family safe. You have the church to protect you. We have nothing. Even the King is not safe." The two discussed the situation well into the night. Finally, Renè reluctantly agreed to his friend's proposal and the next morning Nicolas started his journey back home, still somewhat worried that he had made the right decision.

Nicolas and Jacques were busy all summer securing passage for the family in the spring of 1652. His half-sister Geneviève and half-brother Nicolas Lamarre were also busy preparing for their adventure. The family would travel on to La Rochelle to board the *Volador* under the command of Jean Pointel for the voyage across the Atlantic.

Not one of the travelers had ever seen a ship. It did not take long to find the *Volador,* the smallest ship tied up to the pier! This was the ship that was to take them to New France? It hardly seemed capable of sailing to England. Jacques soon learned the *Volador* would not be alone in the crossing. Three other ships were making a convoy mainly composed of immigrants and cargo. Sailing was set the day after tomorrow.

With cargo stored below decks and crews quarters on the second deck, right below the main deck, passengers had to sleep and eat on the main deck. Because the *Volador* was the smallest there was only one other passenger, a young girl about 14 named Luciene who was a *les filles du roi*. At least Geneviève would have some company.

On April 6, 1652 the *Volador* set sail from La Rochelle. First, the pilot boat was brought along side and lines secured. The topsail gallants were loosened and slowly the sail filled and the pilot boat rowed against the strain of the ropes moving the cargo ship away from the pier. Within the hour the pilot boat was on the way back to La Rochelle and the *Volador* was under full-sail bearing west-southwest heading for her first horizon. All eyes were astern as the coast of France disappeared. There is nothing more frightening than water from horizon to horizon, and a creaky wooden ship being thrust by the wind through churning seas, and your fate and fortune beyond your control.

The 18-week voyage to New France, at first seemed exciting. As the days grew on monotony grew in proportion. The 180-ton *Volador* was barely more than 27 meters (90 feet) in length and at its widest point, amidships was 10 meters. With cargo tied down on the main deck, one had to walk maze-like, through protruding legs and arms of working deck hands just to exercise your legs. A checkerboard had been drawn by chalk on the wooden deck and checkers made from slices of broken mop handle. In rough weather the incoming seas made a mockery of any kind of game by washing away the checkerboard and the pieces. Seasickness that struck the other immigrants did not strike *Volador* probably because of its size. After a few days at sea, one got used to the pitch and yawl of the waves.

At night, the convoy closed to within shouting distance from each other. Now, after dinner, news was passed from one ship to another. Some was important, like water supply and sickness or injury, and some news was gossip. The sister ship to the *Volador* was the *Le Passemoy de Hornen* an older ship that limped along through the waves. The *Volador* being smaller and faster soon gained a one-horizon lead and then more each day. The purpose of a convoy was to stick together, but once at sea, economics took over. The first one to reach port was the first to be reloaded and book passengers for the return trip. Once the *Volador* turned south to avoid icebergs near Greenland, but when the shores of Labrador were sighted, and soon after the green shores of Île Saint-Jean (Prince Edward's Island), both crew and passengers were excited. As the Fleuve de St. Laurent leading to Quèbec was entered excitement rose even further. Soon green grass and rolling hills were viewed on both banks. The next day a fishing boat was spotted – the first sign of life in New France! The *Volador* tied up at the docks in Trois-Rivières, about 60 miles west of Quebec city. The date was June 23, 1652. The *Le Passemoy de Hornen*, commanded by Jean Poulet, tied up five weeks later on August 31, 1652!

In 1652, Nicolas was 57 years old. His wife Jacqueline was 41. Life on the north bank of the St. Lawrence was hard. The hills were not conducive to farming. Nicolas had to look carefully before spending the family fortune on a piece of land. Nicolas and his family moved east up the coast, first to Québec and then unto Chateau-Richer near St. Anne du Beaupre. Jacques asked his father for an advance on his inheritance to purchase a plot of land. Nicolas agreed. Jacques never married and died on November 11, 1681. His final resting place is near the church at Chateau-Richer, Québec, Canada.

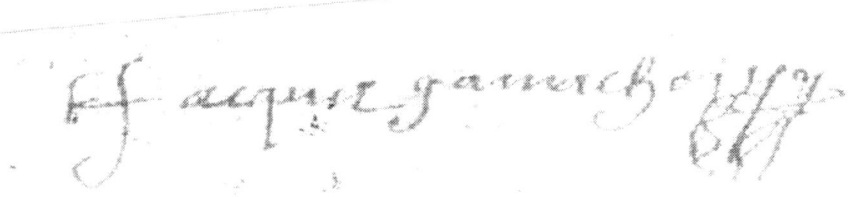

Gamache Family Archives

The signature of Jacques Gamache

On November 11, 1652, four months after her arrival, the young Geneviève, whom Nicolas escorted to New France, married

Julien Fortin Bellefaine, later to become Seigneur (Lord) de Bellefontaine. She was 17 at the time and one of the first brides in New France. Julien was 22. They had 11 children, many of whom became ancestors to the Gamaches of New England. Present at the ceremony were the father of Geneviève and her 13-year-old brother Nicolas Lamarre Gamache, the future Sieur (Sir) de Tardif, along with Louis Gagné, and Claude Bouchard. Father Ragueneau, S.J. blessed the marriage, which took place in the home of Louis Gagné, at Cape Tourmente, which was at that time within the limits of Sainte-Anne's parish. Notary Claude Auber had made the contract of marriage previously at the house of Toussaint on the Cape, August 22, 1652.

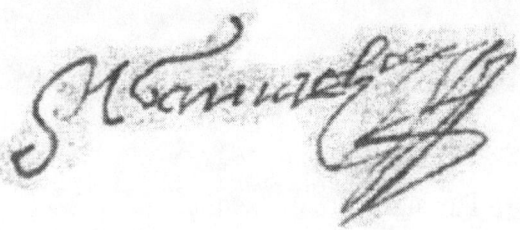

Gamache Family Archives

Nicolas's signature on Geneviève's marriage contract

Julien died in September 1687. Geneviève Gamache continued to live from the inheritance of her late husband, but she would end her days in the home of her son Charles at L'Islet, not far from the fief of her brother Nicolas Lamarre Gamache. She was buried at Notre-Dame de Bonsecours, at L'Islet, on November 5, 1709.

From St. Anne du Beaupre, east of Québec city one can look across the St. Lawrence to prime farmland. Yet the south bank of the St. Lawrence was sparsely settled because a day's ride would put you in British North America! France claimed the land as belonging to New France but the British knew they could settle on the south bank leaving the French on the north bank and the St. Lawrence as a divider. Now there was farmland and plenty of it, thought Nicolas Gamache, but how to acquire it – that is the problem.

The younger Nicolas had taken the job of "chasseur" or "hunter" to Jean Talon, the Administrator of New France. The 75-year old Nicolas would talk to Talon. "I am old. I want to see France once more before I die. Young Nicolas should marry, raise a family, and be prosperous. Being a chasseur is a fine life for someone who is not married. I left France to provide opportunities for him.", said the old Nicolas. Talon listened and said, "Go back to France, I will take care of your son." Jacqueline and Nicolas boarded a ship bound to France in the spring 1672.

Chapter 4

The thirteen old year Nicolas grew to manhood among the hills and fields of Quebec. He was not content to settle down and would hunt weeks on end as far south as the British colonies of New England and New York. When he was in his early 20's his reputation as a hunter got the attention of Jean Talon, the Administrator, who made him *chasseur* (a hunter) for his new fortifications at Québec. When Nicolas was 33, Jean Talon would keep his promise to Nicolas' father, and grant Nicolas Lamarre Gamache, a parcel of land, on November 9, 1672. The grant stated,

"We do hereby certify to one and all that Nicolas Gamache did serve us well and faithfully as personal guide and hunter that we have therefore granted him a concession of land, given him permission to retire at this time to his home and private land, or wherever he chooses to be; we certify furthermore that he gave much proof of his zeal and loyalty; in view of the above, we have signed this document, sealed it with our arms, in Québec, this 9th day of November 1672."

The land grant was for approximately twenty-one acres of the river frontage road, and as a result *chasseur* Gamache became Nicolas Gamache, *Seigneur (Lord) de L'Islet*. The third son of Nicolas, **Nicolas Lamarre Gamache**, married **Elizabeth-Ursule Cloutier** who was born July 28, 1660 in Québec. Prior to the marriage, Nicolas returned home because his father had become ill and died in the summer of 1676. Records show Nicolas re-entered Québec shortly before his marriage on November 9, 1676 in Chateau-Richer, New France. The day before the wedding the marriage contract was signed at the home of Elizabeth's grandparents, Zachary Cloutier and his wife Sainte Dupont. Elizabeth was 16 and Nicolas was 37. Present at the signing ceremony were her parents, Charles Cloutier and Louise Morin, as well as family friends, Nicolas Lebel and Therese Migenault, and the clerk, Gilles Rageot from Québec. Next to Nicolas were his half brother Jacques, his sister Genevieve, her husband, Julien Fortin, and the Fortin family.

  The church ceremony for the newlyweds took place the following day at Chateau-Richer with Father Jean Gauthier de Brullon presiding. Marriages with the French natives were encouraged and some indentured servants, known as *engagés*, were also sent to New France. One such *engagé*, Etienne Trudeau, was the ancestor of future Prime Minister of Canada Pierre Elliott Trudeau. Elizabeth died October 23, 1699 and her husband Nicolas Lamarre Gamache died one week later, October 30, 1699.

Nicolas offered a piece of his land to Monsignor de Laval to build the church of St. Ignace, and he accepted it. The tale of the multiple churches that would be built in the new village of Cap St. Ignace deserves to be told once again. Monsignor de Laval accepted the gift of land from Nicolas Lamarre Gamache, and constructed a wooden chapel near the St. Lawrence. That building rapidly became too small and was replaced around 1721 by a church built of stone. Soil erosion took its toll and on October 29, 1728 the graves of Nicolas Lamarre Gamache and his wife Elizabeth-Ursule Cloutier were exhumed and reburied within the church walls. The 1721 church was washed away by soil erosion in 1744. Again, Nicolas and his wife bodies were exhumed awaiting reburial in a new church.

Louis Gamache, the oldest son of Nicolas Lamarre Gamache decided to build a manor house in 1742. The house was completed in 1744. However, after construction he decided to bequeath the home to the Catholic Church with the stipulation that the church was to be built on Gamache property and all members of his family *in pituitary* could be buried beneath this church.

"On February 25th, 1744, Louis Gamache and his wife, donated land to Cap Ignace for the construction of a new church, before a group of dignitaries. Pierre Rousselot, royal clerk of the south shore, region of Quebec, and resident of Pointe a la Caille in St. Thomas parish, and many other witnesses were present.

Sir Louis Gamache, lord of the fief of L'Illet in the parish of St. Ignace and Madame Angelique Miville, his wife, are duly authorized to establish a new church of St. Ignace, as the one there now is ready to fall into the sea. It is essential to obtain more suitable land on which to build a new church, cemetery and priests' residence. The missionaries and cures of this parish have great need of a new establishment.

Sir Louis Gamache and Angelique Miville hereby authorize of their own free will before the present witnesses, to donate in perpetuity, never to take back no matter what happens, whether debts or other troubles.

Accepting this donation is Monsignor Joseph Romain Dolbec, priest and missionary, now serving in the parish of Cap St. Ignace, accompanied by Sirs Jean Richard, church warden, and Louis Lemieux, also church warden of the old church. Mr. Joseph Romain Dolbec is accepting this donation in the name of the church, as representative of the Bishop of Quebec for the land and for the construction of a new church.

A piece of land two arpents wide and three arpents deep, situated on the fief belonging to the above donators, bordering a ditch, as indicated by markers, bordering the property of Sir Jean Baptiste Gamache on the northeast, and the property of the donators on the southwest. The church, priests' residence, cemetery and adequate surrounding space for many horses will be constructed on this property, to be used and enjoyed by generations to come.

In addition wood for heating from the pine forests will be provided to the priest of this church.

Also, the donators, Sir Louis Gamache and his family will receive a lord's pew on the epistle side of the front of the church in perpetuity, to be passed on to the eldest son of the family. The family will also have eternal rights to receive communion and to be buried in the church, (not the cemetery, but in the church), free of charge.

Accepted this day by Romain Dolbec currently serving the church of Cap St. Ignace and Sirs Jean Richard, warden and Sir Louis Lemieux, warden, and residents assembled for this event. Appropriate vestments and food (pheasants) will also be provided to those in service in Cap St. Ignace church.

Recorded and certified after noon on the 25th of February, 1744, in the presence of Sir Louis Gamache, Sir Jean Richard, Louis Lemieux senior, Jacques and Baril Bernie, Sir Francois Guimon, mayor of Milices, Pierre Fortin, Augustin Bernie, Francois Fortin, Philippe Fortin, Louis Gagne, Gui Cere, Pierre Richard, signed before the above-mentioned clerk. Some witnesses were able to sign, others not. This act was to be read aloud in church several times to make it a completed deal.

Donation made by Sir Louis Gamache and Angelique Miville in the church of Cap St. Ignace on the 25 of February 1744. Paid and registered by the official clerk.

    F. Guimon   Jacques Bernier
    Philippe Fortin   Augustin Bernier
    Guy Cere   Dolbec, priest
          Pierre Rousselet, clerk"

Gamache Family Archives

Translation of the French document establishing the church at Cap St. Ignace, Québec, Canada

This manor house became the rectory for the new church, which was to be located on Gamache land near the center of Cap St. Ignace. However, another landowner, Domaine Vincelotte, wanted the church built on his land further away from the town center. The Bishop sided with Gamache but the church was still in jeopardy. The disagreement would go on for 28 years! Services were held in the Gamache manor. However, since it was not church and no priest was assigned, the sacraments including funerals were not allowed, but took place anyway, and burials in unmarked graves were common near the manor house. These funerals were officiated by a sexton, usually chosen by the parish to lead services in the absence of a priest. Although the Bishop sided with Gamache on the construction of the new church, these burial services were more than he could take and he threatened to excommunicate Gamache if the burials did not cease. That, plus a large contribution by Vincelotte to the church, sealed the fate. The Bishop of Québec City, Monsignor Briand determined that the new church would be built on Vincelotte land. That church opened to the public in 1773 with Nicolas Lamarre and Elizabeth Gamache reinterned. Additions were added in 1824 and 1854. In 1880 the entire building was demolished to make room for a new church. But that church was consumed by fire in 1890. Only the walls on the church survived the fire and the present day church, constructed in 1892, has incorporated those walls.

Gamache Family Archives

Gamache Manor built in 1744. Became a Canadian Historic site in 1959.

Gamache Family Archives

Interior of Gamache Manor
August 14, 1994 250th anniversary

Gamache Family Archives

Street sign near the Manor

Gamache Family Archives

The crypt of Nicolas Lamarre Gamache

What happened to the heirs of Domaine Vincelotte?

Domaine had three daughters! The daughters married and each had no sons!

Gamache Family Archives

Nicolas and Elizabeth with Nicolas's signature

In the seventeenth century, the territory of New France was legally named a Dominion and owned by the Crown. The King of France, or his representatives, distributed parts of land either to nobles, or to rich merchants or professionals, or to people deserving recognition from the State, army officers, for example. These lands were called "seigneuries" or "fiefs", the owner being the "seigneur" or landlord. The landlord had to: 1) "tenir feu et lieu" (build and maintain a manor); 2) distribute lands; 3) declare "Faith and Honor" to the King; 4) produce a required census called "Aveux et Dénombrements"; 5) in some cases pay a required fee to hold such lands called "droit de Quint" or the revenue of one year in others; 6) build a flour mill; 7) reserve oak wood and mines to the King; and 8) reserve some space for roads.

A part of the "seigneurie" remained the domain of the landlord (as a whole or as multiple pieces of land). The rest was divided in "rotures" or "censives" (lots) and distributed to habitants ("roturiers" or "censitaires"). These habitants had to: 1) "tenir feu et lieu" (build and maintain a house); 2) clear the land; 3) build a fence; 4) pay multiple rights to the landlord (rent or cens); 5) keep part of the lot for a road (servitude); 6) reserve some quantities of building or heating wood for the landlord; 7) pay hunting and/or fishing rights; and 8) perform communal work. The "seigneurie" could also contain a communal land where the habitant could send his animals in pasture, while paying a right to the landlord to do so.

The landlord could redistribute part of his "seigneurie" in "arrière-fief" (sub-fief). The owner of this sub-fief became landlord on his own, had the same rights but remained a vassal of the main landlord. It was even possible to redistribute anew a part of the sub-fief as a sub-sub-fief using the same method.

Following sales or inheritance, the "seigneuries" might have many co-landlords. Most of the time, the "seigneurie" itself remained undivided and only the income generated was divided between the co-landlords. The seigneurial system was abolished on December 18, 1854 and replaced with private ownership.

The union between Nicolas and Elizabeth produced ten children. The first-born was **Louis Gamache** (1678 – 1745); then followed Nicolas (1680), Jean-Baptiste (1682), Ignance (1683), Augustin (1686), Elizabeth (1688), Marie Anne (1690), Genevieve (1692), Marie (1694) and Pierre (1698).

Augustin married Marguerite Guyon in 1711. They had one child, Augustin who lived from September 9 to November 7, 1712. His mother died September 15, 1712. On May 28, 1713, Augustin married Louise Caron who was born in 1692. Louise gave birth to twins named Augustin and Nicolas on August 20, 1714 but joy was short lived because both twins died November 15 having only lived a few months. Louise became pregnant again and delivered a daughter, named Louise after her mother, on August 9,

1716. As an 18-year old, Louise married Louis Lemieux November 22, 1734.

Elizabeth (m: 1709) and Marie Ann (m: 1711) married brothers, Pierre (1647 – 1719) and Jean-Baptiste Richard. Pierre was born in Saintonge, France. Pierre was widowed at age 60 in 1707 with six grown children when he married Elizabeth Gamache, 21 years of age. Elizabeth would bear him 10 more children. Jean-Baptiste Gamache married Pierre's sister Agathe on January 8, 1712 but she died in childbirth December 8, 1712.

Gamache Family Archives

Pierre Richard

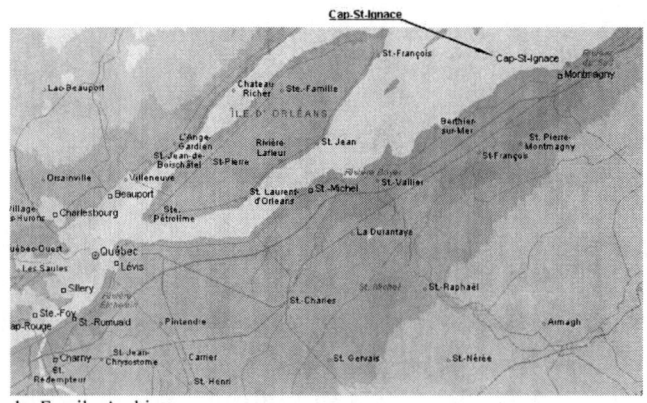

Gamache Family Archives

Cap St. Ignace, Québec

For New France the early 18th century was a period of steady growth. French défrichements ("clearings") spread along the St. Lawrence between Québec and Montreal; the iron forges at Saint-Maurice produced iron for Québec stoves and even cannons; shipbuilding flourished. The colony nevertheless remained largely dependent on the fur trade, which, in turn, depended on keeping the west open.

The expansion of New France in those years was challenged by the outbreak of the War of the Austrian Succession in Europe in 1740's. In Europe, France and England were again at odds over the Austrian Succession, which in turn drew the antagonists into new conflicts.

In North America the war became known as King George's War (1744-48). Fighting broke out again in Acadia, on Lake Champlain, and among the English and French Indian allies in the country of the Great Lakes and the Ohio River valley. It was a confused conflict of raids and reprisals marked by only one action of major significance--the capture of Louisbourg by an expedition from New England.

Holding the St. Lawrence River valley, the Great Lakes, and the mouth of the Mississippi River, the French commanded the better strategic position in America. However, the English colonies, if having a less advantageous location, were far wealthier and more populous.

Chapter 5

These events flavored the life of **Louis Gamache** (1678 – 1745), who inherited his fathers' "seigneur", and married **Angelique Miville-Deschênes** (1683 – 1745) who came from a long line of French aristocrats. Their marriage on April 26, 1702 produced twelve children: Louis (1703), as first-born son, inherited the "seigneur" from his father. The other children were **Jean-Baptiste** (1704); Genevieve Elizabeth (1705); Joseph (1707); Francois (1709); Maria Martha (1710); Ursule (1712); Madeleine (1714); Augustin (1715); Pierre (1716); Ignance Felix (1718); and Michel Arsene (1721). Unfortunately, Angelique died January 8, 1745 and her husband died February 11, 1745 having lived but a short time in the house. Their way of life in New France may well have been buried with them.

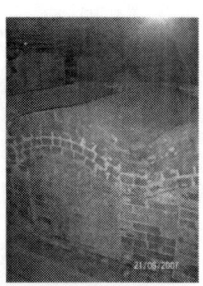

Gamache Family Archives

Crypt of Louis (l) and his mother

The real fall of New France really began in 1689, when the English and Iroquois began a major assault on New France. This war, known as King William's War, ended in 1697, but a second war (Queen Anne's War) broke out in 1702. Québec survived the English invasions of both these wars, but Port Royal and Acadia fell in 1690. Peace came to New France with the Treaty of Utrecht in 1713. Although the treaty turned Newfoundland and part of Acadia (peninsular Nova Scotia) over to Britain, France remained in control of Île Royale (Cape Breton Island) and Fortress Louisbourg, as well as Île Saint-Jean (Prince Edward Island) and part of what is today New Brunswick. England was now in possession of land that would choke off any expansion of New France and they had in the American colonies the population and economic prosperity to ensure eventual victory.

However, France did not die easily because after the treaty, New France began to prosper. Industries, such as fishing and farming, which had failed under the first Governor of Québec, Jean Talon, began to flourish. A "King's Highway" (Chemin du Roi) was built between Montreal and Québec to encourage faster trade. The shipping industry also flourished as new ports were built and old ones were upgraded. The number of colonists greatly increased, and, by 1720, Québec had become a self-sufficient colony with a population of 24,594 people. The Church, although now less powerful than it had originally been, had control over education and social welfare. New France's "Golden Age" often refers to these years of peace, but the aboriginal peoples regarded it as a time of continued decimation of their nations.

Peace lasted until 1744, when William Shirley, governor of Massachusetts, led an attack on Louisbourg. Both France and New France were unable to relieve the siege, and Louisbourg fell. France attempted to retake the fortress in 1746 but failed. It was returned to France under the Treaty of Aix-la-Chapelle, but this did not stop the warfare between the British and French in North America. In 1754, the French and Indian War began as the North American phase of the Seven Years' War (which did not technically begin in Europe until 1756), with the French victory over the Virginia militia contingent led by Colonel George Washington in the Ohio valley.

New France now had over 50,000 inhabitants, a massive increase from earlier in the century, but the British American colonies greatly outnumbered them, with over one million people (including a substantial number of French Huguenots). It was much easier for the British colonists to organize attacks on New France than it was for the French to attack the British. In 1755, General Edward Braddock led an expedition against the French Fort Duquesne, Pennsylvania and although they were numerically superior to the French militia and their Indian allies, Braddock's army was routed and Braddock was killed.

In 1758, Great Britain again captured Louisbourg, allowing them to blockade the entrance to the St. Lawrence River. This was essentially the death sentence for New France. In 1759, the British besieged Québec by sea, and an army under General James Wolfe defeated the French under the General Louis-Joseph, the Marquis de Montcalm, at the Battle of the Plains of Abraham in September. The garrison in Québec surrendered on September 18, and by the next year New France had been completely conquered by the British. The last French governor-general of New France, Pierre François de Rigaud, Marquis de Vaudreuil-Cavagnal, surrendered to British Major General Jeffrey Amherst on September 8, 1760. France finally ceded New France to the British in the Treaty of Paris, signed on February 10, 1763.

Chapter 6

Jean-Baptiste Gamache, the second son of Louis was born in 1704.

Gamache Family Archive

Baptismal record of Jean Baptiste Gamache
May 8, 1704

May 8th, 1704

On this day of May a son was born from the marriage of Louis Gamache and of Angelique Minville, his wife, residents of this parish. On May 8th I baptized this child as missionary of the parish of Cap St. Ignace and he was given the name of Jean. His godfather was Eustache Fortin and his godmother was Anne Le Mieux, wife of Charles Bernier of this parish. Eustache has signed this document, the godmother was unable to sign, and I am recording this according to church doctrine.

    Eustache Fortin   Father Pierre Lepoivre, missionary
Gamache Family Archives

Translation of the Baptismal record

He married **Elizabeth Bazin** on November 15, 1730. Elizabeth was born in La Durantaye, Québec on January 16, 1710.

Gamache Family Archives

Marriage certificate of Jean-Baptiste Gamache and Elizabeth Bazin
November 15, 1730

"November 15, 1730
On the 15th day of the month of November, 1730, after having published their bans three times and announcing them during parish masses, on October 29, on All Saints Day, and on Sunday, November 5th, a marriage was performed between Jean Gamache, son of Sir Louis Gamache, lord of this parish and of Lady Angelique Miville, his father and mother, one hand, and Elizabeth Bazin, daughter of Francois Bazin (deceased) and resident of la Durantaye, and of Francoise Cadrin, her father and mother, on the other hand. As no impediment was found to prevent this union, I, the missionary signed below of St. Ignace, having received the mutual consent of all parties to this wedding, have given them a nuptial blessing according to the laws of our mother the Holy Church, in the presence of Sir Louis Gamache, father of the groom, and of Louis, Joseph and Francois Gamache, his brothers, of Nicolas and Jean Gamache his uncles, of Sir Eustache Fortin, Francois, Philippe, Jean and Louis

Fortin, cousins of the bride and several other guests, some of whom have signed this document with me as official recorder.

   Eustache Fortin   Ignace Caron   Francois Xavier Caron
Father Simon Foucault, missionary"
Gamache Family Archives

Translation of the Marriage Certificate

Their marriage produced eight children: Jeanne Elizabeth (1733), **Jean-Baptiste** (bapt.1734),

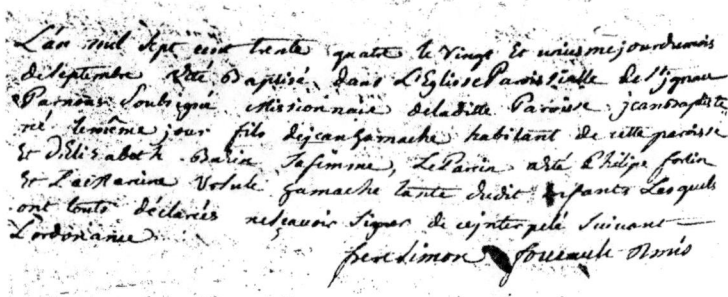

Gamache Family Archives

Baptismal Record of Jean-Baptiste Gamache, September 21, 1734

"September 21, 1734
On this date of September Jean-Baptiste Gamache, born this very day, was baptized in the parish church of St. Ignace by the parish missionary, signed below. Son of Jean Gamache, resident of this parish and of Elisabeth Bazin, his wife, his godfather is Philippe Fortin and his godmother is Ursula Gamache, his aunt. As they were unable to sign, signing the record in their name.
    Father Simon Foucault, missionary"
Gamache Family Archives

Translation of Baptismal Record

Joseph Marie (bapt.1736), Nicolas (1737), Augustin (bapt.1739), Jean (1742), Marie Claire (1744), and Madeline Marie (1746). In 1748, only three years after his parents death, Jean-Baptiste Gamache died after having lived for only 44 years and was buried in the churchyard at St. Ignace.

Gamache Family Archives
The Internment of Jean-Baptiste Gamache January 18, 1749 in a sepulcher

"Jean Gamache died November 15, 1748
Entombed January 18, 1749

On January 18th of the year 1748, Jean Gamache, age 45, who died on November 15th of the preceding year, was entombed in the cemetery of the above mentioned church and the ceremony was presided over by the undersigned missionary priest of St. Ignace. Jean Gamache was buried the day after his death in the Gamaches cemetery, and his body was moved to the church cemetery in January. The above named Jean Gamache died without the final sacraments being administered by the church. Attending the burial ceremony were M. Hiche, attorney of the King in this New France,

and Mr. Louette, recorder of the admiralty. Also present is Mr. Vincelotte, lord of this parish, who signed the document with me.
                      Father Curot
Vincelotte du Hautmesny   Hiche
   Louette"

Gamache Family Archives

Translation of Internment Certificate

The son, Jean-Baptiste (called Bapbette by his family) and his mother Elizabeth, along with his seven brothers and sisters, sat in the expanded house that Louis had started in 1744. They gathered around the table, having just come from his father's funeral. Bapbette was 15 years old. Being the oldest son meant Bapbette now had to shoulder responsibilities his mother was saying. "Are you listening, Bapbette?" his mother asked. "Yes, of course, I have to be more responsible." he agreed, as he walked over and picked up his father's 50-caliber flintlock. "I'm going to need this if I'm going to be responsible to feed the family", he stated assertively. He was trying to feel important, and his ploy must have worked because his mother nodded her head in agreement.

Bapbette's grandfather Louis, who brought more property near St. Ignace, had sold the homestead that Bapbette's great grandfather received from Talon. Together Louis and Bapbette's father had nearly 60 arpents (50 acres) along the river road. This was good land and rich soil. Bapbette liked to go down to the river because on a clear day one could see the coast line of Îsle d'Orleans which someday he hoped to farm.

Like his great grandfather, his grandfather, and his father, Bapbette was a farmer and a hunter. Living across the river and east of Québec meant two things. First, the best hunting for deer and beaver were to the South towards British New York. With his father, Bapbette had been as far South as the area around Fort Ticonderoga visiting Iroquois villages trading for furs. He knew his knowledge of the rivers and Indian paths would be valuable some day because the British and French had been fighting for over 50 years. Fifty years was small potatoes.

The British and the French have been at each other's throats for seven hundred years! One can scarcely imagine the depth of antagonistic feelings between the French and British. Remember it was William the Conqueror, King of England who burned Mantes-a-Jolie in 1087. William was the Duke of Normandy! A Norman! The bastard son of the Duke of Normandy! But, to the French, he was a contradiction. A bastard Frenchman and an English King! Perhaps that started the rivalry between these two great countries. But nothing would equal the gamesmanship played out on the chessboard of the North American continent.

In 1740, the population of the British Colonies in North America was approximately 890,000 roughly eight times that of New France. Within 20 years the British population doubled! In the next 10 it doubled again! New France and Québec were doomed.

After 1682 when La Salle claimed all lands west of the Allegheny Mountains to the Pacific Ocean for France, French dominance continued until the end of the French and Indian War in 1763. France, not Britain nor Spain, lay claim to most of North America that we know today. The American colonies were spread up and down the East coast. They were blocked by further expansion West by the French. England needed to defeat the French, in Canada, and drive them out of North America. Early in the war, the French forces were victorious with British forces surrendering at Fort William Henry in northeastern New York. However, on September 13, 1759 on the Plains of Abraham, above Québec the British defeated the French and, through the Treaty of

Paris in 1763, France ceded Canada and all North American territory east of the Mississippi to England! The French kept New Orleans.

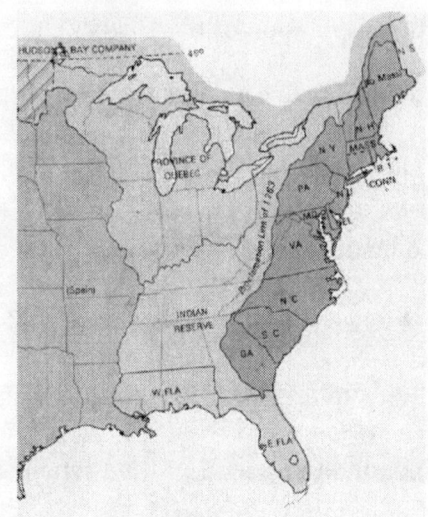

Gamache Family Archives

Québec Province in 1763

How France lost their holdings west of the Mississippi was more intriguing. During the 16th and 17th centuries France and Spain had, to say the least, strained relations. But, through marriage, in 1700's, the new King of Spain was a Bourbon! The Grandson of Louis XIV! France, desirous of ending the bitterness sought to make amends by resurrecting the previous Treaty of Utrecht, which gave Newfoundland and Nova Scotia to the British. A secret Treaty of Fontainebleau was attached which now gave Spain most of the lands west of the Mississippi. This effort in 1763 hoped to avert more wars and difficulties. By stroke of the pen, across the Atlantic Ocean, France lost two-thirds of what we know call the U. S., retaining only New Orleans. However, because of political reasons, Spain, trying to keep the treaty a secret from the British, did not exercise control over their new land until 1768. Another secret treaty actually returned all lands to France and by 1803; President Thomas Jefferson would purchase 880,000 square miles of land (Louisiana Purchase) for $15 million. This completely strangulated France. Thus, in a few short years, lands bordering the Mississippi River had three flags – French, Spanish, and U. S. These events play themselves out in the founding of St. Louis!

Meanwhile, Bapbette farmed and grew into manhood in St. Ignace. He lived at home, took his mother to church, and afterwards stopped to pray at his father's grave. He joined the militia, which fought in the Great War (1756 – 1759). He was a Captain in the militia fighting along with the French General the Marquis de Montcalm. He was there when the Marquis was fatally wounded on the Plains of Abraham above the city of Québec.

It was a humiliating defeat for New France. At the Treaty of Paris in 1763 France surrendered all military and political power in North America. For Bapbette, life would never be the same. He did not wait for the inevitable to occur in Paris. He left Québec in 1762. His mother had married a widower, Joseph Godrau on February 4, 1758. All his brothers and sisters were grown with families of their own.

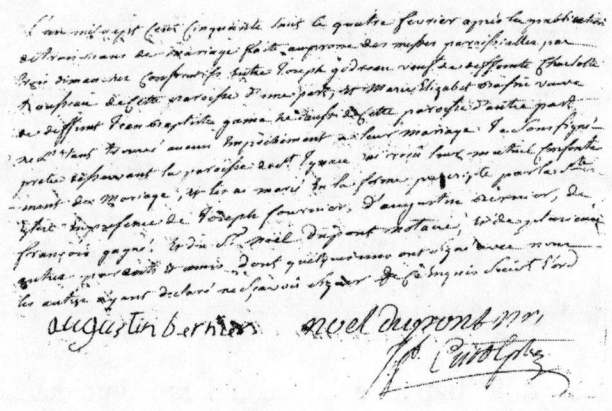

Gamache Family Archives

Marriage Contract Between Joseph and Elizabeth

"February 4th, 1758
On this date, after publishing bans three times during parish masses on three consecutive Sundays, a marriage ceremony was performed between Joseph Godreau, widower of Charlotte Rousseau (deceased), on the one hand, and Marie Elisabeth Bazin, on the other hand, widow of the deceased Jean Gamache of this parish. No reason to prevent this marriage being found, I as the undersigned priest of this parish of St. Ignace, and having received their mutual consent to this marriage, married the couple with appropriate ceremony of the Holy Church, and in the presence of Joseph

Fournier, Auguste Bernier, Francois Gagne, and of Sir Noel Dupont, clerk, and several other relatives and friends, some of which signed below, and others of which declared themselves unable to sign, official recorded this day...

Augustin Bernier   Noel Dupont, clerk   J.F Curot, priest"

_{Gamache Family Archives}

Translation of the Marriage Recording

With his share of money from the sale of his father's farm he set off through French territory, with perhaps the intention of reaching the last French strong-hold in America – New Orleans. He picked out the best horse from his father's estate and packed two saddlebags with the meager possessions he would need, 50 musket balls, powder, several small flints for his musket and one pistol, one large flint for making fire, five pounds of dried venison, a dozen apples, one rabbit trap, and a whetstone for sharpening knifes. In addition he had a bedroll and a wood canteen belonging to his father, which was filled with buttermilk. His brother Joseph gave him a wine bota made from goatskin. In case his aim was bad while hunting, his older sister Jeanne dried some peas to eat and wrapped them in a big blue cloth. No extra clothes and no toiletries were taken since people only bathed twice a year, in June and November.

Bapbette was 28 years old when he left Québec for the last time. From the hills five miles away from his home he could barely make out the Îsle D'Orleans. Trees had long obscured the red roof of the house his grandfather had started and his father had lived in for such a short time before his death. As he turned back towards the woods little did he know what great adventures lay in store for him as one of the founding fathers of the city of St. Louis!

While he had been to Maine, New Hampshire, Vermont and New York on hunting trips with his father, he had enough of the British and decided to stay in the Province of Québec until he arrived at Fort de Chartres on the Mississippi.

He headed southwest staying on the south bank of Fleuve de St. Laurent. The first day he arrived in the evening at mission of Saint Joseph de Sillery where he stayed the night. Fortified by breakfast the next morning he set out for a two-day journey to Trois-Rivières, a French fort and trading post. There, it was good to have companionship to discuss politics, fur trading and Indian affairs. Most of the fur trading occurred between St. Laurent Iroquoi a tribe that had not joined the Five Nation Confederacy. The Confederacy who sided with the British during the French and Indian War lived to the south of Luc Ontario – only a foolhardy Frenchman would venture into their lands!

South of Trois-Rivières was a ford where the St. Laurent narrowed to a few hundred yards and Bapbette crossed over to the north shore and continued his southwest journey to Ville-Marie (Montreal). Ville-Marie and Quebec were the two major cities in New France. Both were bustling out-posts with ships tied up to the piers, warehouses full of goods from Europe, and inns with real French wines. It was tempting to stay in Montreal but in order to get to New Orleans Bapbette must move on because the most dangerous part of his journey lies ahead.

On the south shore of Luc Ontario lived the tribes of the Five Nations. The Seneca, Cayuga, Onondaga, Oneida, and Mohawk. Best Bapbette stays on the north shore protected by the Wyandotte, whom the French called "Huron". "Le huron" means "wild boar" in French and the mohawk haircut of the Huron reminded the French of the bristles on a wild boar.

Author's Note: The Wyandotte word for village is "kanata" which gave Canada its name. Today, most Canadian Wyandotte speak French.

Staying north of Luc Ontario Bapbette encountered numerous small Wyandotte's villages. Rather than encroach on the villages hospitality, Bapbette preferred to set up camp alone.

Once the horse was unsaddled and groomed for the night he was tied to a tethered rope and allowed him to graze. Bapbette liked the early evening in the woods. Animals were settling in for the night, birds were singing their last goodbyes, and the forest was quieting down for the short summer night. Bapbette was baking corn meal in a covered pot to eat with his dried venison and cleaning his ever-present musket. After dinner, he gathered pine needles and moss to make a bed. Sunrise would come in a few hours.

Bapbette continued on his west-by-southwest trek until he reached a Huron village then he spent two days with the Huron before he continued southwest to Detroit River, staying in Québec (now Ontario) the winter of 1762.

In the spring, he crossed the Detroit River and stayed three weeks at Fort Detroit. There he met the Commandant Alphonse deTonty who said his daughter, Marie Josephè de Tonty, and his 14 year-old granddaughter Charlotte, left in the fall for Fort de Chartres accompanied by his new son-in-law Pierre Tremblay. (Charlotte would marry Bapbette in 1767 in St. Louis!)

Commandant Tonty was the brother of Henri de Tonti, an Italian by birth, soldier, financier, and fur trader in the employee of France. In 1682 accompanied René Robert Cavelier, Sieur de La Salle, or Robert de LaSalle, explorer of the Mississippi, made history by claiming all the lands west of the Appalachian mountains to the Pacific Ocean for France. Marie Tonty married Louis D'Amours on 26 April 1745. Louis died near Fort de Chartres in 1755. Marie and her 9 year-old daughter returned to Detroit. Marie married Tremblay in 1757 and now has journeyed back to Fort de Chartres. Bapbette agreed to pass letters to each when he arrived at the Fort.

> **Author's Note**: The brothers continued to spell their last name differently, one preferred to Italian spelling (Tonti) and one the French (Tonty).

Jean Baptiste Gamache left Detroit the Monday after Easter and arrived at Fort de Chartres (Illinois) the fall of 1763. While at the Fort he met Pierre Laclède, who had just brought his wife, Marie Thérèse Bourgeois Chouteau, and her 12 year-old son Auguste, to live with him.

Fort Chartres, at the time of Bapbette's arrival was already an old established fortification. The first and second forts were made out of timbers which burned but a third fortification built a few miles distant was made of limestone which had been quarried near the Mississippi.

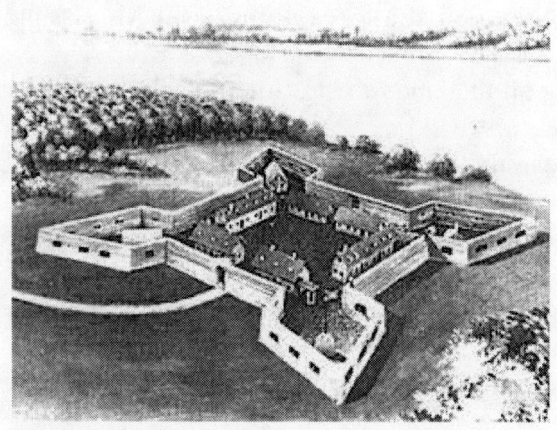

Gamache Family Archives

Fort Chartres

Gamache Family Archives

Main Gate, Reconstructed as a WPA project in the 1930's

Gamache Family Archives

Swivel Gun Located Above the Main Gate

Gamache Family Archives

Officer's Quarters

Gamache Family Archives

Fort Chartres in Winter

The history of the Fort Chartres area of southern Illinois, 60 miles south from what was to become St. Louis, is interwoven with New France's history and that of the Indian tribes who lived in the mid-west area including the Missouri area eastward to the Ohio valley.

French explorers Father Jacques Marquette and Louis Jolliet, visited the area in 1671, when the tribes of the Illini Confederacy occupied the St. Louis area. This loosely organized Confederacy included the following tribes: Cahokia, Kaskaskia, Michigamea, Moingwena, Peoria and Tamaroa. They spoke a common language and were all related by blood. At the time of first contact by the

French, they were already in possession of some French trade goods received in trade from tribes like the Ottawa.

Father Gabriel Marest, a French Jesuit priest who mastered the Algonquin dialect of the Illini, organized a combined Indian-European settlement in 1700 at the mouth of the River Des Peres north of what is now St. Louis, Missouri. This included Illini from the Kaskaskia and Tamaroa tribes. The settlement included cabins, a chapel, a crude fort and native structures. Because of fear of an attack by the Sioux, traditional enemies of the Illini, the Indians of the Des Peres settlement in 1703 moved to the east side of the Mississippi near the mouth of the Kaskaskia River. Finally, the settlement moved to Fort Chartres in 1720's.

Chapter 7

In 1764, Laclède, his 14-year-old ward Auguste Chouteau, along with 27 men, including Jean-Baptiste (Bapbette) Gamache, set off from Fort de Chartres. They crossed the Mississippi and headed north. The Treaty of Paris in 1763 has ceded all the lands from the right bank of the Mississippi, and East to the Appalachians to the British. The left bank of the Mississippi was still under French control. The only settlement on the left bank was St. Geneviève, which was an outpost with buildings too small to hold Laclède trade supplies.

Previously, Laclède had stopped at St. Geneviève while heading north out of New Orleans in 1763, but discovering the lack of facilities there, pressed on to Fort Chartres having been offered by the Commandant there, sufficient storage for his trade goods. Being depleted during the winter, the stores were down to a manageable size, Laclède departed to find a new location on the west bank. Their original landing site was the confluence of the Missouri and the Mississippi but it proved to be too marshy so they picked a site 18 miles south. Laclède named the outpost St. Louis after the sainted King of France. The date was February 15, 1764.

Pierre Laclède, who sometimes added the family name "Liguest" at the end of his signature to identify him from other relations, was born in 1724 in Bedous, France. He served in the army and arrived in New Orleans in 1755 as a "gentleman traveling for pleasure." He was well educated and known for his skill in fencing.

He fell in love with Marie Thérèse Bourgeois Chouteau, a woman whose husband had abandoned her in New Orleans with a young son. Laclède made the boy, Auguste Chouteau, his ward and a clerk in his office. Because French and Spanish law, and the Catholic Church, forbade divorce, Laclède and Madame Chouteau maintained a discreet relationship, but she became his common-law wife and they had four children together Jean-Pierre (1758), Marie Pelagie (1760), Marie Louise (1762), and Victoire (1764) Chouteau. These children were baptized as the children of Madame Chouteau's legal husband, René Auguste Chouteau. René Chouteau was in fact in France having escaped from authorities in New Orleans after battering then abandoning Madame Chouteau.

Laclède became interested in the fur trade, and in 1762 received, along with Antoine Maxent, the exclusive right to trade with the Indians of the Mississippi and Missouri Rivers. Laclède returned to St. Louis in April 1764 with a design for the town, where his 14-year-old ward Auguste Chouteau was overseeing clearing of the land. Soon, he sent for Madame Chouteau who was residing at Fort Chartres with their children.

Madame Chouteau was an astute businesswoman who once sued her own son Auguste, for money lost when a slave of hers had been killed while working for Auguste. Pierre built her a house and office that became the fur company's headquarters with cabins for the men and storage sheds for provisions and tools. The post house, completed in September 1764, was located on the block once bounded by Market, Walnut, First and Second Streets which is now part of the Jefferson National Expansion Memorial Park. The house became the nucleus around which the village was built and also the focal point for all measurements locating lots and streets.

As laid out by the French, the village contained three north-south streets, La Grande Rue (Main Street), Rue d'Eglise (Church Street) and Rue des Granges (Barn Street); now First, Second, and Third Streets. There were several narrower east-west streets including La Rue de la Tour, Rue de la Place and Rue Missouri; now

Walnut, Market, and Chestnut Streets. In addition to the block for the post house, squares were set aside for a church and a public place. A fort was built on the hill overlooking the village, at what is now the area of Fourth Street and Walnut Streets. Attacks from Indian populations were always a concern.

At the time the French first encountered the Illini in 1671, their numbers were estimated at 3,800-4,000 warriors, they were regarded as the "masters of the Mississippi". By 1787 there were only about 50 Illini surviving in Illinois. In 1794, about 100 Peorias were living ten miles south of St. Geneviève at a place known as *Bois Brulè* (burnt woods). This group had perhaps 40 warriors. Even at this late date, Chickasaws from the South were still continually attacking them. As late as 1803, a number of Peoria Indians lived inside St. Geneviève, Missouri, which provided them some protection from raids.

Chapter 8

Jean-Baptiste (Bapbette) Gamache settled down and married the love of his life, **Charlotte D'Amours (de Louvière),** the daughter of Marie Josephè (Tonty) Tremblay, born in Prairie du Rocher, Illinois near Fort de Chartres in 1746. The marriage took place according to church records on May 3, 1767 in St. Louis.

The Gamache Family Archives is fortunate to have a copy of the marriage contract between Charlotte and Jean-Baptiste dated in 1767, and is one of the earliest legal documents in St. Louis's history. Joseph Labusciere whose signature appears at the bottom of the last page wrote the marriage contract in French. There were two learned men who would perform such a task.

The first was Joseph Lefebvre d'Inglebert des Bruisseau who is commonly called Joseph Lefebvre. He was a native of France and he came to New Orleans in 1743, and to Fort Chartres in 1744, having obtained from M. de Vaudreuil, Governor General of Louisiana, a grant of an exclusive right to trade with the Indians on the Missouri. After his trade privilege was given to others he served as judge of civil cases at Fort de Chartres for a number of years, and came to St. Louis with St. Ange. Lefebvre died in 1767 about the same time as the marriage contract was written.

His successor was Joseph Labusciere. Labusciere was a notary and the King's le *procureur*, or attorney, an important personage always, under the French law, and of course most important in the eyes of the early French settlers of the Mississippi valley. All the early documents in the Missouri State Archives, except the first fifteen written by Lefebvre, are in the handwriting of Labusciere.

Labusciere was a resident of St. Louis for twenty-five years, connected officially with the government at first, afterwards legal adviser and attorney of the people, who prepared their legal papers; a person of consequence, useful and valuable to the village. During the time that St. Ange administered the government, he was custodian of the archives; and countersigned land grants. Between April 20, 1766 (the first marriage contract) and May 20, 1770, Labusciere prepared one hundred and forty-four papers of various kinds. Generally, the documents deposited in the Missouri State Archives relate to sales of lots, sales made under executions or to bonds and obligations assumed, bargains and trades and engagements for services as well as sixteen marriage contracts.

Mary Gamache, Tucson, Arizona, and Gisele Alias of Lyon, France, made a translation of the marriage contract that revealed some interesting facts. Gathered together as witnesses for Jean-Baptiste and Charlotte were family and friends. They included some of the earliest citizens of St. Louis. Jean-Baptiste Martigny, Françoise Moreau, Pierre (Tonty) Tremblay, Pierre Belestre, and Louis Deshêtres were in attendance as well as Charlotte's mother Marie Josephè and Charlotte's sister Thérèse Marie D'Amours (de Louvière).

Jean-Baptiste Martigny and his brother Joseph were both fur traders, born in Quebec and both attended the ceremony. Jean-Baptiste married Hélène Herbert from Fort Chartres and built a stone house on the corner of Main and Walnut Streets in present day downtown St. Louis. That home would later become the Government House.

Francois Moreau was a merchant and landowner who married Catherine Marechal. In 1796, he received a grant of land near St. Ferdinand. He also claimed in the grant to pay in full a bad debt of François Poillivre on the banks of the Maramec. In 1797 he opened a boarding house and built a house for his family that was later turned into a park. He also owned four arpens (about 200 acres) on the Mississippi near St. Genevieve that contained a mine.

Pierre Picote Belestre was a soldier and fur trader. He was born in Montreal, migrated south and stayed at Fort Chartres and finally came to St. Louis.

Charlotte's mother was Marie Josephè Tonty and her family called her "Josy" or "Josette". She was the niece of Henri de Tonti who accompanied La Salle on his explorations of the Mississippi in 1682. She was born May 27, 1713. Her father was Alphonse de Tonty who was born February 17, 1689 in Montreal. Alphonse was Commandant of Fort Detroit and one of the Founding Fathers of Detroit, Michigan. Josy's mother was Anne Picote born about 1693. Since Pierre Belestre's middle name is "Picote", the same as Josy's mother's maiden name, there is a strong possibility they are related, perhaps nephew and aunt.

Josy's first marriage to Louis Bertin D'Amours (de Louvière) occurred on April 26, 1745. Louis was born July 16, 1698 and died January 21, 1755. The D'Amours family goes back to

1300's and is related to the King's of France. After her husband's death in 1755 she married again on April 18, 1757 to Pierre Tremblay, who also was in attendance at the marriage between Jean Baptiste and Charlotte. Pierre Tremblay was born October 11, 1736 probably in Detroit. He signed the marriage contract with "Tonty Tremblay".

Also in attendance was Charlotte's sister Thérèse Marie D'Amours (de Louvière). She was born in 1748. Louis Deshêtres attended the marriage contract ceremony as an interpreter because Thérèse could not understand Spanish. (St. Louis had transferred to Spanish control after the Treaty of Fontainebleau. The marriage contract was written in French and the Roman Catholic marriage ceremony was certainly in Latin, but knowledge of Spanish would be important.) Louis and Thérèse must have turned their relationship into romance because Thérèse married Louis Deshêtres in Detroit on February 18, 1770!

Some explanations are needed for French legal terms used in the marriage contract. The contract cites the "Common Law of Paris". In France in 1760's each province developed its own common law called "le cutume" which translates as "legal practices born from local customs." Ultimately, Napoleon centralized French law with his Civil Code effective March 21, 1806. The French, in early St. Louis history, adopted the Common Law of Paris for their transactions. Finally, a "Clause de Precipit" is the clause often introduced into marriage contracts through which the couple stipulates that in case one of them dies suddenly the survivor has the right to take a certain sum of money from the estate to pay for final expenses of burial and to exist until the estate is probated. The following is the English translation of the marriage contract.

"Document 2013. The Historical Society, State of Missouri, St. Louis City Archives.

    Being present Jean-Baptiste Gamache, adult male, approximately 30 years of age, inhabitant residing in port St. Louis. Being the French party (descent), son of the deceased Jean-Baptiste Gamache and of Elizabeth Bazin, his father and mother, natives of Cap St. Ignace, government of Quebec in Canada. Also before us, as representative and as married woman, Josy B. Tonty, widow of the deceased Mr. Louis d'Amours from Louviere, standing up for Miss Charlotte d'Amours de Louviere, the young lady here present of her own consent.

    This couple, upon the advice and counsel of their relatives and friends assembled here and named below, acquaintances on behalf of Jean-Baptiste Gamache, Mr. Alexis Picard, resident, and Mr. Rene Kiercerau, also a resident, his friends, standing in for his absent parents. On behalf of the above-mentioned young lady Charlotte d'Amours de Louviere, are the above named Dame de Tonty, the widow Louviere, Mr. Louis Deshêtres, interpreter of the nations (meaning he was interpreter of Indian languages and also English because Thérèse, Charlotte's sister did not understand English), and Thérèse d'Amours de Louviere, her sister. (Also present were) Mr. Jean-Baptiste Montigny, (French army) officer, living in St. Louis, (and a) cousin of Miss Louviere and Mr. Francois Moreau also residents and relatives of the young lady are all witnesses to the advice and counsel of the relatives and friends named below and assembled here, all have made and agreed to this marriage contract which follows this page.

May it be known that the Dame widow Louviere has promised the above mentioned Miss Charlotte Louviere, after swearing that she is her daughter, to Jean-Baptiste Gamache, who has promised to take her for his legal wife and to celebrate their wedding before our mother the holy, apostolic and Roman Catholic Church.

Stating what will be done with their goods and what each will require of the other in (their) marriage. All goods, furnishings, and household property, will be held, by the couple, in accordance with the Common Law of Paris. This common law of Paris will continue in effect and will regulate the affairs of their household even if they should move their household to a far-away land (Quebec) where the common law is different than the common law of Paris, which is used here. Neither party shall be held responsible for any debts held by the other party before the wedding, and if such are found, they will be paid off and taken care of by the person who incurred them.

These two persons take each other in matrimony with all of their goods and rights belonging to them at this time and with those which might come to them in the future, whether from their parents as gifts or otherwise, and which will become part of their household. Holding in reserve those items, which are excluded from the whole by the common law of Paris and according to which their household will be operated.

And from the sincere love felt by the mentioned future spouses, is given a dowry to the future bride of seven hundred (silver) pounds, as dowry prefix, paid once, as well as a part of all goods and earnings of her future husband enjoyed during his lifetime and legally his. These sums may be inherited by any children, which might be born of this marriage in the future. The above-mentioned future spouses (will) set aside the sum of three hundred fifty pounds to go to the survivor as well as all goods and furnishings inventoried as part of their household. (This would be a clause de precipit.) The above-mentioned sums of dowries, and sums of money up to the choice of the survivor, will be available to any future children of this marriage and to the future wife.

The bride surrenders claims to all which she has brought to the marriage, whether as gifts, or as dowry payments, as all will now become part of their holdings as a couple and she declares herself to be free of debt and eligible to receive one day the above amount in the clause de precipit.

Concerning debts incurred by the future household, and because of the sincere and reciprocal love that the future couple holds for one another, these following are to be put in place. All goods, furnishings and "immovable" (property)…(this could mean the house or land), will be inherited one day, by any survivor, in full ownership.

This mutual gift is made with the consent of Dame Tonty, the widow Louviere. If there should be no children born of this marriage, this gift from Dame Tonty will be null and void.

Witnessed by those present here today, agreed to and instated, is this agreement between the promised parties and agreed to by Jean-Baptiste Gamache in the home of Mr. Louis Deshêtres where the future bride is residing, in the year 1767, on May 3rd.

In the presence of the here-mentioned relatives and friends and in the presence of Father Francois Louis Belatre, and of Jacques Marechal, clerk of the register and of those who have signed here and also on behalf of those witnesses present who have not signed this day.

Father Belatre   JB Montigny   Tonty Tremblay
 Marque X Gamache   Marque X Charlotte Louviere
Rene Kiercerau   Marque X   Louis Deshêtres   Labusciere
(Jacques Marechal wrote in the X signatures.)"
Gamache Family Archives

Translation of the French Marriage Contract

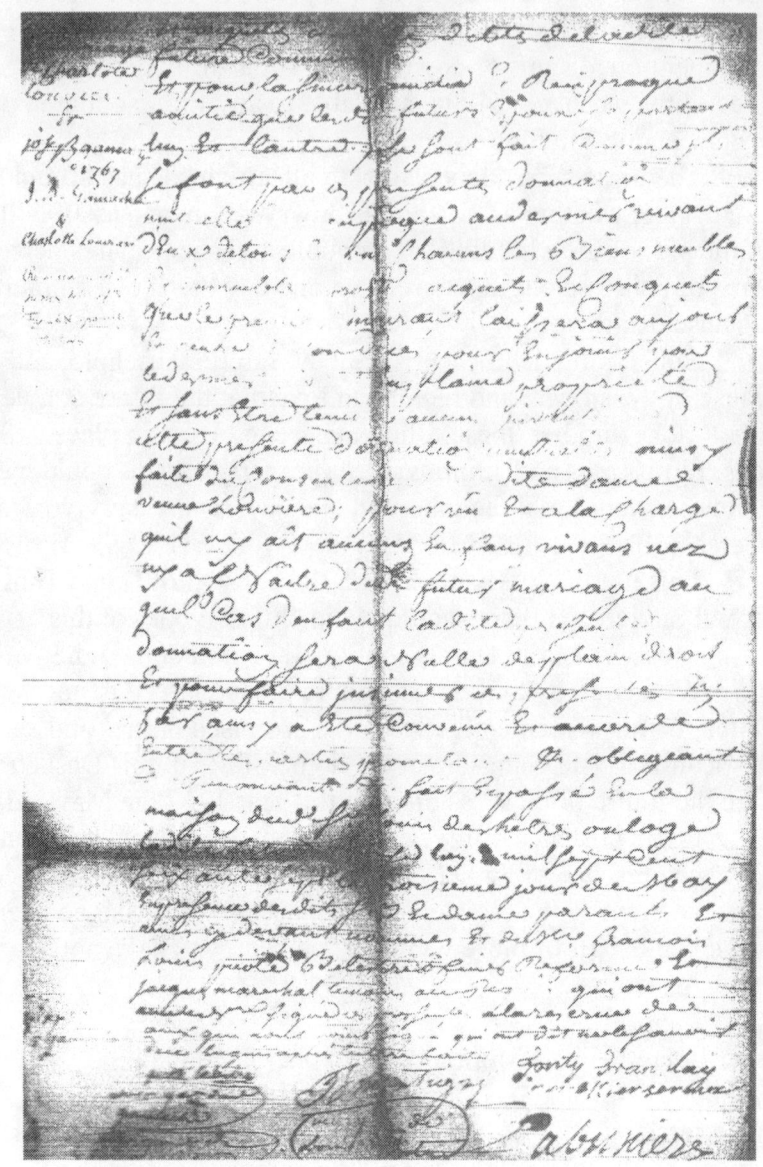

Gamache Family Archives

Signature Page of Marriage Contract

Jean-Baptiste and Charlotte had six children: **Jean-Baptiste** (1768); Marie Joseph (1772 who died in infancy); Augustin (1774); Marie Theresa (1776); Louis (1778); and Francis Xavier (1780 – born in St. Genevieve and died four years later in St. Louis). Bapbette died April 17, 1805 at 71 years of age. He was buried with his sisters' Jeanne large blue cloth. The one she carefully wrapped dried peas when he began his journey. It had been saved all these decades as the last memento of his Québec days and his wife had stitched in a border that read, "Je me souviens", "I will remember." He saw the city of St. Louis grow under three flags, French, Spanish, and the United States.

Bapbette was originally interned at St. Louis, King of France Cemetery (also called the Old French Cemetery) at 3rd and Walnut Street near the Old Cathedral close to the Arch to the West in downtown St. Louis. His burial spot was less than a stone's-throw from land he owned, which is now the northern foot of the Arch. His wife, Charlotte who died twenty-four years earlier in August 23, 1781 was buried in the same cemetery. The bodies were then moved to the Old Catholic cemetery due to construction of downtown St. Louis. That cemetery was located at 2nd and Market. Again due to construction the bodies were removed to the New Catholic cemetery then to St. Bridget of Erin Catholic cemetery, 2401 Carr Street. Their final resting place is Calvary cemetery, Section 5, listed as "Unknown" because records have long been lost. It is ironic that the founders of St. Louis, Laclède lies in a unmarked grave on the Arkansas river, Jean-Baptiste Gamache lies in Calvary in an unmarked grave, and who knows about the rest of that first landing party. How little respect we pay to those brave pioneers who gave us such a great city. There ought to be a monument!

    Laclède gave Jean-Baptiste a "verbal land grant" in 1765. This plot of land was enough to build a house 20 feet by 25 feet. Each person built what was called a "post house"; staking out the four corners of the "house" until such time as construction began. The recording of these "verbal grants" were to be made later by the Commandant of Fort Chartres, who was the French administrator of the area. The Commandant, following the British assumption of command, left Fort Chartres for New Orleans, leaving his second in command, Captain Louis St. Ange de Belle Rive, who because of his position was also the Lieutenant Governor of Louisiana.

Soon after the British took possession of Fort Chartres in 1766, Captain St. Ange moved his garrison to St. Louis and established civil and military control of the city.

On the 27th of April 1766, he made the first land grants affecting property in St. Louis. When these land grants were made, prior claims to plots were recognized; so the first settlers, including Jean-Baptiste's verbal grant, were recorded. St. Ange required the land grants to be recorded in the "Livre Terrien" or Register of Deeds.

> **Author's Note:** The original *Livre Terrien* is located in the National Archives in Washington, D.C. St. Ange and Laclède's actions are later open to question because at that time the secret Treaty of Fontainebleau had been in effect since 1763 giving Spain all the lands west of the Mississippi. Their land grants were useless according to arguments before the U. S. Supreme Court in reclaiming portions of Gamache lands. In defense it was pointed out that they did not know their actions were illegal since France gave the lands west of the Mississippi to Spain by the secret Treaty of Fontainebleau. Nobody knew of the treaty at the time. The lands were acquired back again by the secret Treaty of San Ildefonso during Napoleon's reign. Six weeks later, Napoleon sold Louisiana to the U. S. in 1803. Jurisdiction was a term used quite liberally since residents of the area were not informed of the shifts of political fortunes as they occurred.

Thus custom of verbal land grants was continued after the Spanish obtained dominion over the territory in 1768 and until the Louisiana Purchase in 1804. In 1766, St. Louis consisted of 75 buildings and about 300 inhabitants. The design of the village followed the French town system, which provided for a town on a small tract divided into small square blocks, each block individually owned by a "habitant."

Another basic problem was a provision for land suitable for cultivation, known as a "Common Field." The common fields were owned by individuals and were long, narrow strips of land laid out side by side. It is said that this design was adopted as a safeguard against Indian attack, enabling the settlers to work the strips in a line, keeping together in a more secure position. The original common field extended from Market Street on the south in present day St. Louis to the large mound at the foot of Mullanphy Street on the north, and from Broadway west to Jefferson Avenue. This tract was divided into farms, which were one or two arpents wide (an arpent being 192 feet six inches), with a depth of forty arpents or 7,700 feet.

The houses in the village were built either of stone or of timber posts set on end in the ground. The stone was quarried along the river bluff, and the site chosen was well wooded so timber was in abundance. The wealthier settlers erected the stone houses. The architectural style was similar to that prevailing in the South. The houses were one story in height with a loft above and steeply pitched roofs on all sides. The larger ones had porches or galleries all around, others galleries only in front.

The numerous timber structures were built of round posts set about three feet deep; some of the better ones were made of hewn posts about nine inches square set on a stone foundation wall about four feet above ground level. The majority of the houses were about twenty by thirty feet in size, divided into two or three rooms. Some consisted of one large all-purpose room with an outside kitchen shed. The stone houses usually had fireplaces in each room and hand-hewn flooring. The first church building was a log structure built in 1776 on the same block now occupied by the Old Cathedral.

In 1770, at the end of St. Ange's administration, the village contained 15 stone houses and 100 wooden ones, of which about 75 had been erected during 1765 and 1766. The population numbered

500. In the 1776 census of St. Louis, Jean-Baptiste Gamache (Bapbette) and his wife Charlotte are listed along with their family.

In 1769 Antoine Maxent dissolved his partnership with Laclède, who then made Auguste Chouteau and Sylvestre Labbadie his partners. Laclède fell deeply into debt and was in poor health by 1777 when he traveled to New Orleans to try to straighten out his fortunes. While traveling back to St. Louis on May 27, 1778, Pierre Laclède died on a boat anchored just two leagues below the Arkansas Post on the Mississippi, and was buried in an unmarked grave.

St. Louis owed its very success to the flourishing trade with neighboring tribes, especially that with the Osage. The Osage were famous for the quality and quantity of deerskins supplied to St. Louis traders. It has been estimated the tribe harvested 100,000 deerskins in a single year. Deerskins, and other skins of fur-bearers, were big business in St. Louis. Deerskins alone were so important because they could be used to make clothes and moccasins, which were the predominant style in early St. Louis. Plus they fetched competitive prices in markets in Montreal and New Orleans. There was so much demand for this commodity in St. Louis' first forty years of existence, deerskins functioned as the unofficial currency for purchasing just about anything in the community. As such, the Osage nation was very important to the early economy of this river community.

Chapter 9

Bapbette's son, who was also called **Jean-Baptiste** (III), was born in 1768 and died in 1839. His marriage to **Catherine Marguerite Constant,** born in 1773, took place on November 12, 1787. She died May 21, 1833. Both are buried in St. Louis, King of France cemetery. They had eight children: The oldest son was **Jean-Baptiste** (IV) (bapt.1790). A second son was born in 1791 named Gabriel. The rest of the family included Euphrosine (1794); Joseph (1796); Nicolas (1800); Catherine (1805); and Louis David (1808).

Author's Note: As you have discovered, the Gamache clan were not inventive in naming children. The same names keep cropping up from generation to generation. In order to keep the lineage orderly, I have devised a system for numbering the Jean-Baptistes. The first Jean-Baptiste whose father was Louis Gamache is (I). His son Jean-Baptiste (who is named Bapbette as a literary device) born in 1734 is (II). His son Jean-Baptiste born in 1768 is (III) and his son Jean-Baptiste is (IV). What is confusing to genealogists is these are not all the Jean-Baptiste Gamaches in existence! Many of the other sons also named the sons after the father's father – Jean-Baptiste! Fortunately, Jean-Baptiste (IV) changed the pattern, and the son to whom the author is related is Pierre.

Bapbette's son, **Jean-Baptiste** (III)**,** had a difficult life. In 1833 Catherine, Jean-Baptiste's wife died and two years later Gabriel, his second oldest son died.

Gabriel married Emily Solomon, born December 2, 1802 and they had two children, Gabriel, Jr. born in 1828 and Samuel, born in 1832. After Gabriel's death, his brother Louis David, by now a Justice of the Peace, was appointed "estate guardian" of the children, Gabriel, Jr. and Samuel, ensuring they received their fair share of Gabriel's estate. Emily later married Jean Boucher thus forfeiting any claims to Gabriel's estate.

Jean-Baptiste (III) was the administrator of Gabriel's will and two items are of interest. Upon death, as was the custom, all possessions were sold – including the wife's clothes! A wife was considered "property" and everything belonged to the husband. Everything had to be inventoried. Then a date was set aside for the "estate sale", by auction, to the highest bidder. Family records show the wife bought back some of her own dresses! The second point of interest was the "auction" was a big social event. Friends, neighbors, and family gathered for the auction. According to Gamache Family Archives, Jean-Baptiste, probably wanting to ensure a good sale, bought whiskey – for the price of thirty-seven and one half cents. It is interesting to note the contents of a man's possession in the 1830's.

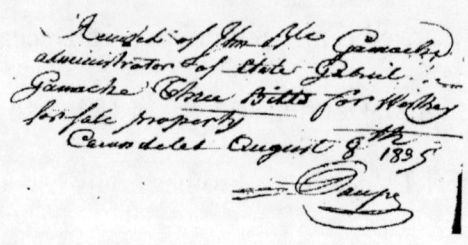

Gamache Family Archives

Bill for whiskey

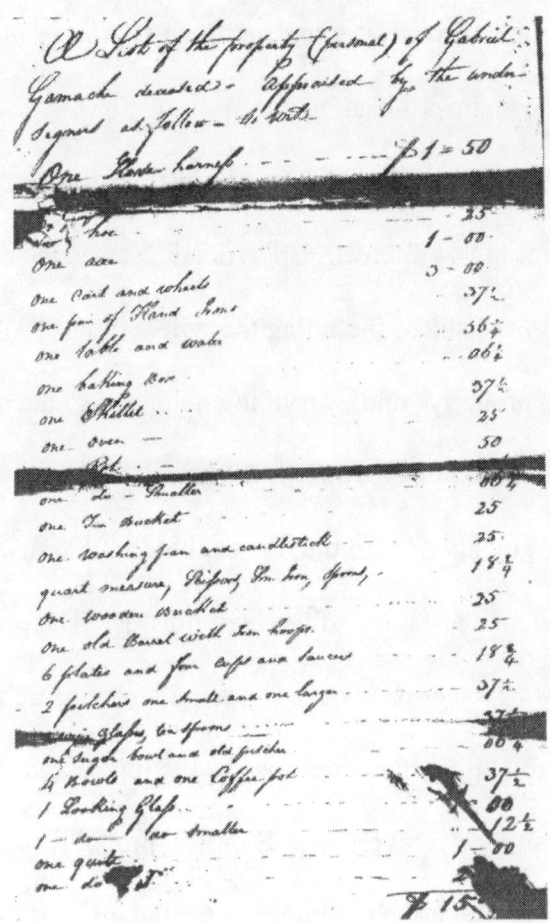

Gamache Family Archives

Inventory of Gabriel's Possessions (Continued of next page)

```
Amount brought over -        $  15 - 37½
One Calico Counterpane               2 = 00
One  Cotton   do                        25
3 Sheets (cotton)                  1 - 50
2 furnitures of the lower part of a bedstead   37½
2 pillows ... cases and one ...           
One woman Cloak                          
three women's frocks              3 - 00
three  do   shirts                      75
two   do   shirts and one old frock    62½
1 Woollen Shawl                         50
1 Cotton  do                            25
5   do    handkerchiefs                 25
One Woman's Bonnet and Comb             50
One man's hat                      1 - 25
2 Waistcoats                            
3  do   and Suspenders                 12½
3 yards of Col. cotton                  75
2 man's Shirts                     1 - 50
One Soldier's Cloak                     25
One Cupboard (walnut)              8 - 00
One feather bed                   10 - 00
One bedstead                       6 - 00
One mare                          25 = 00
two chairs                              
                                   $ 83
We the undersigned have appraised the above
articles to the best of our knowledge this 9th day of
August 1835            John + Bouche
```

Gamache Family Archives

Inventory of Gabriel's Possessions

A List of Gabriel Gamache's property Sold to the highest bidder this 8th day of August 1833 —

One horse harnep — Thos Chartrand	$2-00
One Spade — Peter Delor	87½
One hoe, Joseph Chartrand	37½
One axe, John Pouraly	1-18¾
One horse cart and wheel, Benoist Marechall	4-12½
Hand iron, Mr Salomiak Gamache	43¾
One table and watui, Louis Guion	50
One baking box, Thos Chartrand	25
One Skillet, Domingue Eige Sr	68¾
One Oven — Ignace Pason	75
One pot — Ignace Byon	87½
one do Smith, Pouraly Eige	37½
One Tin Bucket, Leon Lery	37½
One washing pan and candle stick, Sangram Michau	31¼
quart measure, Sifors, Pr Son and Johns B. Marechal	31¼
One wooden bucket, St Amant Michau	56¼
one barrel with Iron Hoops, Domingue Eige Sr	35¼
6 plates, 4 Cups and Saucers, Mr S. Gamache	25
2 pitchers — Joseph LeBlond	37½
5 wine Glasses and tea spoons Joseph Bonyn	1-00
one Sugar bowl and one pitcher, Ant Guion	12½
four bowls and Coffee pot, Ant Guion	43¾
1 Looking glass, Benoit Marechall	1-18¾
1 do Shaler, Sangram Michau	31¼
1 quilt — Peter Delor	1-37½
1 do — John Pouraly	3-75
	$23-12½

Gamache Family Archives

Inventory of Items sold (continued on next page)

81

[Handwritten inventory document - Gamache Family Archives]

Gamache Family Archives

Inventory of Items Sold

The ploy of Jean-Baptiste to pry the auction bidders with whiskey evidently paid off because the items sold for much more than appraised! The Gamache Family Archives contain probated wills, land sales, and notes that reflect life in the 19th century.

Chapter 10

Jean-Baptiste Gamache (IV) was christened, according to church records, on September 4, 1790 and died on July 5, 1846. He is buried in Sts. Mary and Joseph Cemetery established in 1775 and located between 2nd and 3rd Streets in Carondelet. Carondelet was an independent municipality at the time; however, since 1876 when St. Louis City split with St. Louis County it was absorbed into the city.

Jean-Baptiste (IV) had a most interesting life. According to church records, when the existing timbered church was destroyed by fire in the 1830's, he contributed to rebuild the church, which was dedicated in 1834. Now called "The Old Cathedral", it is the site where many of his children were later baptized. Nearby was the church cemetery where his grandparents are buried, but the cemetery, on the corner of Walnut and Third is no longer in existence, and the Archdiocese is unsure where their remains have been relocated, if at all. Jean-Baptiste (IV) was a farmer, trapper, road builder, and most importantly, for me, a father.

He married twice. The first wife was Brigette Riviere, born January 1, 1793, whom he married on June 14, 1813. They had two children: Brigette (1820) and Octavia (April 29, 1823). It is reported in the Gamache Family Archives that Brigette, his first wife, died August 10, 1823, possibly as a result of complications resulting from childbirth. She is buried at Sts. Mary and Joseph Cemetery in Carondelet.

His second marriage was to **Françoise Vien** who was born November 1803. Jean-Baptiste and Françoise Vein were married in a civil ceremony in 1824 and later married in the Catholic Church January 29, 1827. They had eight children: **Pierre** (later called Peter) (1825); Marguerite (1828); Francis (1830); Emilie (1832); Françoise (1834); the twins Maria Marie and Edward (1838); and Eliza (1840).

> **Author's Note**: With Jean-Baptiste (Bapbette) (II) through (IV) the Gamache family has more documentation concerning their lives and fortunes. First, they lived during a time in which public records were kept. A multitude of records, including federal and state census and court documents were recorded; but vital statistics such as birth and death were not recorded until the 20th century. Church records recorded births, baptisms, deaths, and burials, and were often used in place of government records, or to substantiate missing records.
>
> Robert Parkin reconstructed a 1776 census of the twelve-year-old village of St. Louis at the time of the bicentennial. The reconstructed census indicates 1,297 men, women, and children were living in St. Louis. There were 115 in the Catholic

Church graveyard. Records such as the Catholic Church register, militia rolls of 1780, and Spanish Archives, including the French *"Livres Terrien"* (land books) and civil marriage contracts, were used in compiling the file of original settlers as well. The 1776 census of St. Louis was also consulted.

In the original *Livres Terrien* in the National Archives in Washington, D. C., Jean-Baptiste is listed as owning land, which is located where the northern leg of the Gateway Arch stands today.

Jean-Baptiste Gamache (II) is listed in the 1776 census as a farmer, age 43, who was born in Québec. His wife is listed as Charlotte, age 30, who was born in Prairie du Rocher, Illinois. The children are: Auguste age 2, Jean-Baptiste (III) age 8, Marie Joseph age 4, and Marie Therese born June 8, 1776.

All Jean-Baptistes (II) through (IV) were landowners, farmers, speculators, and businessmen. Late in the 18th century, St. Louis and St. Genevieve had become trading posts of considerable importance, but the country lying between was filled with warring Indians and wild animals, thus making an overland journey between these two points extremely hazardous. Francisco Cruzat, who was the Lieutenant-Governor of Spanish Upper Louisiana, desirous of removing the perils of the journey, offered a donation of 1,050 arpents of land (approximately 892.5 acres) to anyone who would establish, keep, and run the ferry across the Meramec River.

Jean-Baptiste (Bapbette) (II) accepted the offer and established a ferry across the Meramec River, at what is now known as the Lower Ferry. For this service, he was granted a tract of land at the mouth of the Meramec, which includes the present day bridge across the river and what is now Jefferson Station of the St. Louis Iron Mountain & Southern Railway.

At the same time, a trail was marked out on the west side of the Mississippi from St. Louis to St. Genevieve, passing lengthwise through what is now Jefferson County. This trail was called "the King's Highway" or *El Camino Real*. It crossed the Meramec at the ferry and was the first highway marked out in Jefferson County.

Around 1789 the Spanish government established a road that ran from St. Louis to Little Prairie, now Caruthersville, MO, turning south through Campo de la Esperanza, Arkansas. The greater part of its course followed an old Indian trail along which de Soto probably traveled. After 1850, this route became known as Telegraph Road because the first telegraph in Missouri followed the route with the first poles embedded in the old trail.

Years later the ferry was sold to Jacques LeMais (the city of Lemay was named after Jacques) and LeMais moved operations upstream a little (Lemay's Ferry). The corner of St. Louis County at the Meramec is called "The Point."

Jean-Baptiste (II) cultivated his 1,050 arpents of land until 1780 when he was ordered away because of Indian disturbances. Other land owned comprised a "league of land" (approximately 6,000 acres) comprising 90% of the corporate boundaries of Arnold, Missouri, including Jefferson Barracks.

The story of Jefferson Barracks is filled with stories of swindle and intrigue. Jean-Baptiste Gamache (Bapbette) (II) owned the land that was passed down from generation to generation by probated wills or deeds. The land became Jefferson Barracks in 1826. This was a portion of the 1,050 arpents from the Spanish land grant. However, the original land grant was never found at the time. In 1930's the original grant was located in a monastery in Piernas, Spain.

The Louisiana transfer left St. Louis land titles in a chaotic state because the concessions by Captain Louis St. Ange and succeeding Spanish governors were not formalized into written royal grants. Instead, the French citizens in St. Louis relied upon neighborly trust and a handshake to confer title. This system was ripe for abuse. When the opportunity presented itself to record a written deed the Jean-Baptiste's (II) through (IV) did not do so. Yet, Gamache Family Archives consist of many recorded deeds and assorted legal papers. The process of recording deeds seems to have been unfortunately selective! To some degree, one has to look at the world from their historical perspective. First, the land they occupied was Spanish, then French, then Spanish again, then French, with an immediate sale to the United States under the Louisiana Purchase. Governments come and go but farming stays the same. So, a parcel of land is sold for a pig and everybody is happy except the pig! Why should a person ride 20 miles to see a lawyer to draw up a deed, ride to the courthouse to record the deed, and ride back home? We own this land! A handshake will do. Besides, in time some other government will claim this as their land! Secondly, there is so much land – just build a house and farm the land – it is yours for the taking. Well, soon, that attitude betrayed the owners. Unscrupulous individuals took Jean-Baptiste and others to court to confiscate the owner's lands. All during the 19th century, in Missouri and elsewhere, money could be made by land speculation. Collet's Index to Instruments Affecting Real Estate recorded in St. Louis

County, Volume 1, Part II, Grantors F – M, has two and a half pages devoted to the Gamache family real estate transactions.

A rumor started after the War of 1812, after the British burned the White House in Washington, D. C., that the capitol was too vulnerable to attack and ought to be moved to the center of the country – the area south of St. Louis – land owned by Jean-Baptiste Gamache.

The frenzy of land speculators converged, supported by the American authorities who annulled previous verbal claims. Only those claimants who could prove actual settlement and cultivation had their claims confirmed by Board of U.S. Commissioners. The Commissioners rejected 70% of all claims to prime land. Even though, according to the Land Claims in Missouri, U. S. Congress, in the Second session of the 23rd Congress, Docket No. 197, Case No. 145, unanimously upheld the claim of Jean Baptiste (II) to the original 1,050 arpens, that decision was later overturned.

Less then one year later, in 1836, President Polk decreed that the land grant to Jean-Baptiste Gamache was not recognized by the United States since the property was not improved, nor surveyed, nor farmed. Even though Jean-Baptiste had sworn witnesses to attest to the fact he cultivated and farmed the land, he still lost his claim. The land was too valuable to the U. S. government to be claimed by one man. The Commission gave the property to land speculators who sold it to the city of Carondelet, who than sold 1,700 acres of Jean-Baptiste's property to the federal government for the sum of-------five dollars. Gamache sued and the case went all the way up to the U. S. Supreme Court – three times – (See Appendices B and C)

The original "deed" to Jefferson Barracks stated it was to be used as a military reservation "as long as it was needed" then revert back to its previous owners or their heirs. Presently, there is a federal cemetery at Jefferson Barracks (there are 15 Gamache grave markers) and a museum, but it is no longer an active base. In the 1950's part of the Jefferson Barracks land was turned into a Historical Park.

Gamache Family Archives

Entrance to the Park

Gamache Family Archive

Jefferson Barracks Historical Park

In the 1920's the Gamache family sued the U. S. government to try to regain their land. Of course the government won. But as late as the 1970's Gamaches still were hiring lawyers to appeal. Governments twist statements to their advantage, lawyers collect monies with only minimal work, and those who pay lose hard earned money.

Back in St. Louis, 1842, Erastus Wells began the first transit operation. The city streets were first illuminated by gas in 1846, and the police department was organized. That same year, the Mercantile Library was incorporated.

In 1843 Judge William Primm sold a plot of land facing Michigan Avenue for $400 to Julian Gamache, a cousin, who was a carpenter and planing mill proprietor. Gamache built a home on the property, which is still standing today. With its 14-foot high ceiling and grand staircase it represents one of the finest antebellum homes in St. Louis.

Jean-Baptiste Gamache (IV) died without ever seeing his claim settled. We are fortunate to have a copy of his will written in 1841 giving all his worldly possessions to Françoise Vein Gamache, his second wife. The last 20 years of Jean-Baptiste's life was spent in courts trying to prove he owned the land where Jefferson Barracks stood. Even after death, the courts tied up the probation of the will until 1849 by which time Françoise had moved to Stringtown, St. Louis County, (a town which no longer exists having been absorbed by St. Ferdinand, later absorbed by Florissant) where she was almost destitute. Family records show she petitioned the court to relieve her of the duties of executrix of Jean-Baptiste's will because she was poor and in ill health but the petition was denied. Those who scammed Jean-Baptiste were relentless towards his widow. She appeared on the 1850 census but since has disappeared. No one knows when she died or where she is buried.

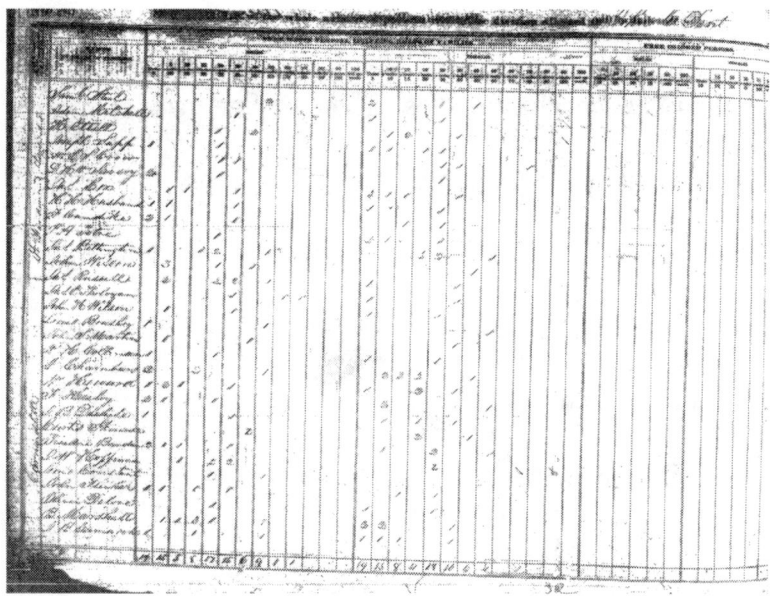

Gamache Family Archives

1840 Federal Census, Saint Ferdinand, St. Louis County, showing Jean-Baptiste Gamache (b. 1790) and family

Early census, either federal or local, was notoriously inaccurate. For example, in the census above, Jean-Baptiste (b. 1789) is shown on the last line above the page totals. When Gamache Family Archives are matched up with the census you can obtain a clear understanding of this line. First represented are males. You will notice one male child in the first column, which is birth to 5 years of age. This would be Edward, born in 1838. The next mark is in the column of 15 – 20 year old. This would be Pierre (Peter) who was born on May 26, 1825. Next you have a mark for Jean-Baptiste in the 50 to 60 column, because he was born in 1790 according to Gamache archives. Then the first mark under the female column is Eliza, born in 1840. The second mark, 5 – 10 years of age should have been 2 rather than 1 since Maria (b. 1836) and Françoise (b. 1834) should have been displayed. Marguerite (b.1828) is next, followed by her mother, in the 30 – 40 column because she was born in 1803. Two children are not listed in the census; Francis and Emile died in infancy.

Received from Mrs Des Gamache the sum of two Dollars and a half ($2.50) for the digging of a grave in the Church yard "

Carondelet August 6th 1846.

Jn. Bte Chatillon

Gamache Family Archives

Receipt for digging the grave of Jean-Baptiste Gamache

Gamache Family Archives

The French will of Jean-Baptiste Gamache written in 1841

Know Ye by these Presents, that I John Baptist Gamache of Carondelet in the County of St. Louis State of Missouri, being sound of mind, memory & natural acquirements, attending & seeing to my business, & knowing that there is nothing more certain than death, the hour uncertain, & wishing before passing from this life to another, to dispose of the few goods & chattels which it has pleased God to vest me with. I have to this effect ordered (redacted) & named the present writing my testament, to wit: Firstly, I wish my debts to be duly paid, if there be any. Secondly, I declare to have been married in first wedlock to Brigitte Kiercere, of which the living fruit of matrimony is Maria. 3rdly, I declare to be lawfully married to Frances Vien, my beloved wife, of which marriage there are living at this day six children, to wit: Peter, Margaret, Eliza, Agnes, Edward, Bridgette, & should there hereafter be an additional number, I wish & order that they be considered on the same footing with those above mentioned.

4ly) I give & bequeath to my above named beloved wife, all my furniture, cattle, horses, hogs &c, cooking utensils, & money which may be found, or belonging to me, on the day & hour of my demise, to enjoy, do & dispose of as though her own real property, without any difficulty or discount whatsoever.—

5ly) I give and bequeath to my above named beloved wife, my lands, lots of common & town, which may belong to me at the day of my death, that she may enjoy, do, & dispose of, & draw the revenues thereof, during her widowhood only, rents & profits for her benefit, but, to be well understood that if at her death, or if she be again joined in matrimony, that then, the above grant, of lands, lots of commons & town, are to be considered as null & void, & may be divided among my heirs above mentioned, & to those who may legitimately be born hereafter.

6th) I nominate as executrix of my present will, my above named beloved wife Frances Vien, that she fulfil my will in regard to my heirs according to my will rejecting & annulling all other wills, codicils, powers or other dispositions that I may have made previous to the present, my full intention & last will, to be read & re-read, declaring & asserting my voluntary act,—Made, signed & sealed by me at St. Louis, in the above County this twenty seventh of July, in the year of our Lord eighteen hundred & forty one.—

Witness
H. Rexard
Theodore Papin
M. P. Leduc

John Baptist + Gamache (Seal)
           his mark

Gamache Family Archives

Translation of the will

An inventory of the Estate of John Batis D Gamache Deceased

1 horse .. 1 horse Colt .. 1 Black mare .. 2 Colts ..
1 yoke of oxen .. 1 Cow & Calf .. 1 heifer .. 1 Cow .. 3 ploughs
1 pair of traces & Swingletree .. 1 harrow .. 2 Matakes ..
3 howes .. 1 log chain .. 1 Cook stove .. 1 Small Stove 3 Bedsteads
3 Beds .. 2 Cupboards .. 3 tables .. 1 Shot gun .. 1 Clock ..
1 Big kettle .. 6 chairs .. 1-2 horse waggon & harness ..

1 Well .. 1 deed from L P gamache to J B Gamache $700
1 deed from the Commissioners in favor of J B gamache in
St Louis County Recorded in Book 7 page 62 .. 1 deed
from J B gamache Sien to J B Gamache Jr 60 arponts more
or less St Louis County Book M page 254 & A duplicate for
The same .. 1 deed in the Common Lot of Corondelet Jr $93
from the Citizens of St Louis to John B Gamache
1 Mariage Contract J B gamache Bergette Rivera
1 deed Assy to Gale & Wife to deed to J B gamache 30 arpts
in the common field of Corondelet Recorded Book u pay
page 148 .. 1 lot claim deed dated April the 19th 1821
1 Receipt of one hundred dollars
peter gamache to J B Gamache
1 Receipt peter delor to J B gamache 100 dollars
Cash in hand 15 dollars

James T Jones
Francis Boly

I do hereby Certify that the foregoing inventory
of the personal property of
John Bt Gamache is Correct and true
so far as the Same has come to my Knowledge

Sworn to and Subscribed   Francis Gamache
this 2d day of September   mark
A D 1867.   J H Clincere

Gamache Family Archives

Partial Inventory of the Possessions of Jean-Baptiste Gamache (b. 1790)
Showing His Father (b. 1768) Deeded Land to Him

Chapter 11

Pierre, also called Peter, (1825 – 1900), mentioned in Jean-Baptiste's will as the son, lived with Françoise at Stringtown with his wife **Josephine (Josette) Pigeon** whom he married on January 18, 1844 two years before his father's death. They had six children: John Baptiste (1848); Peter (1849); Brigit (1850); **Oliver L.** (1857); Alexander (1853); and Andrew (1859). Evidently Josephine died around 1860 because Pierre married Mary Dillon, born 1833 and an Irish immigrant, November 30, 1862. They had eight children: Francis (1863); Edward George (1866); Mary Josephine (1869); Marguerite (1870); Bridellia (1872); Magdaline (1874); Tobias Julian (1875); and Anna (1877). In the last year of the 19th century, April 2, 1900, Pierre, who insisted his surname was "De Gamache" died at 310 Ellwood Street at the age of 84 and was buried under that name in Mount Olive cemetery, St. Louis. Mary (De Gamache) died on February 14, 1910 and is also buried at Mount Olive.

Gamache Family Archives

Mary Dillon and Pierre (Peter) Gamache

Gamache Family Archives

Pierre (Peter) De Gamache

Gamache Family Archives

Mary (Dillon) De Gamache

François (Frances) Gamache 1850 Census

Author's Note: The first introduction to Nancy May occurred on the Internet. Pierre was also her ancestor. Subsequently, she and her husband Charles visited with the author in Williamsburg, VA, where she contributed Pierre's and Mary's photograph.

Gamache Family Archives

Nancy May

Peter would walk the streets of Carondelet in the 1890's and engage passersby in conversation about "the old days" when his father owned the land where Jefferson Barracks is located and how the government robbed the family of its fortune. This scenario was related by a former slave discussing, through oral history, the early days of Carondelet and recorded in the State Archives. Much of Pierre's life is a mystery. We know he married twice, lived with his mother at Stringtown, but not much else. Actually, we know a little bit more about St. Louis at the end of the 19th century.

A cultural factor in the growth of St. Louis was the Agricultural and Mechanical Fair, established in 1855 in what is now Fairground Park. Beginning as a small county fair, it gradually grew into a large exposition, of more than 100 acres in area, with pavilions devoted to the arts and sciences, a zoological garden and a racecourse. Its reputation became international, and American presidents and European royalty traveled to visit it. The fair was held in the fall of each year and attracted hundreds of thousands of visitors to the City, many of whom remained as residents. Perhaps Peter and Mary took the family to the fairgrounds. Perhaps it was there that his portrait was taken.

A new type of power for transit appeared locally in 1886, when the St. Louis Cable and Western cable car line began operations. It ran from Sixth and Locust Streets to Vandeventer Avenue via Franklin Avenue. During the next year a cable line was placed in operation to the Fairgrounds. Cable cars enjoyed a short but profitable period of operation before they were supplanted by the faster electric trolley car in the nineties. In 1887, several street railways were authorized by the city to use electricity as power for the operation of cars. The principal operating companies of this time were the Lindell Railway Company which ran to the west end, the Union Depot Railway Company which operated in south St. Louis, and the Mound City line which covered most of the north side. Most of these transit firms were consolidated in 1899 into the St. Louis Transit Company, which initiated a universal transfer system.

Railroad connections in St. Louis were coordinated in 1889 with the Terminal Railroad Association, which controlled all railroads entering the city from the east and west. It had taken over operation of Eads Bridge and Merchants Bridge and the railway yards in 1893. During the early 1890's it began construction of the new Union Station, which was the largest in the world when it opened in 1894.

St. Louis grew at a more leisurely pace during the last two decades of the 19th Century, although subdivision activity continued at a healthy rate during the 1890's. In the 1890 census St. Louis regained its fourth place among American cities with a population of 451,770, and the number of telephone subscribers climbed to 2,885.

Chapter 12

Oliver Lee Gamache (1857 -1921) was the author's great grandfather and the son of Pierre. He married **Madora (Dora) Tesson** May 6, 1880. Dora was born September 15, 1861 and died June 23, 1911. She is buried at Sts. Peter and Paul Cemetery in St. Louis. This is a pauper's grave, with marker 02529, registry entry 63720. The cemetery, established in 1865, is located on Gravois Blvd. in St. Louis about 7 miles from the court house.

Gamache Family Archives

Dora's gravesite

Upon visiting Sts. Peter and Paul cemetery in St. Louis and attempting to locate Dora's grave, I decided to buy a small headstone, which I hope will be a comfort to her.

Oliver was 22 years of age and Dora was 19 when a Justice of the Peace in St. Charles County married them. Less than a month later, they both appeared on the 1880 U. S. census of Portage Township. Also on that page of the census her father and mother appeared. Her father Isaac Tesson was 69 and her mother Mary was 41. Dora died in 1911 after a long illness.

Dora Tesson was a fascinating woman. The Tesson family and the Gamache family were associated with each other for many generations. At 60 years of age, Honoré Louis Tesson, Dora's grandfather, came from Quebec to St. Louis in 1792 and worked the Gamache ferry across the Merimec. Later, Honoré would build his own ferry, and Tesson Ferry Road in South St. Louis is the route to his enterprise. The word Tesson, in French means a badger. Perhaps, some member of the family resembled a badger!

Dora was very superstitious; and once she would not move into a house because a window shade rolled up unexpectedly – a sign, she thought, that somebody had died there. She used to gather medicinal herbs in the woods for treating sick neighbors. Grandmother Daisy remembered her, and would tell stories about her to her oldest grandchild, my brother Rynard. She last worked as a cashier and lived in a rooming house on North Sarah Street with Mena, the widow of Joseph Gamache. Her husband Oliver is buried at Mount Olive cemetery in St. Louis, Section 1, Lot 0304NH.

Author's Note: The notation "NH" signifies "No Headstone"

Gamache Family Archives

Marriage recording of Oliver and Madora

Gamache Family Archives

Oliver Gamache's Death Certificate

Gamache Family Archives

Madora Gamache's Death Certificate

Oliver and Dora had three children: the author's grandfather **Joseph Lee** (1881); Cecelia (1886); and Oliver Lee, Jr. (1894).

Nancy May's grandfather was Oliver Lee, Jr., the brother of the author's grandfather. Oliver, Sr. and Jr. were notorious drunkards. One night, before World War I, they decided to change their middle name to Pierre. They did not know how to go about it legally but decided they had a right to call themselves by whatever name struck their fancy. One family "rumor" is that an ancestor named "Pierre" was more French sounding, and this would aid in the Jefferson Barracks suit (probably Pierre who was called Peter most of his life but returned to "Pierre" when circumstances warranted such a move). The family wanted to be as French as possible to win any suit! After all, Oliver's father was called "De Gamache"! So, their "middle names" were sometimes "Lee" and sometimes "Pierre", depending on how much they had to drink! Obviously no mention was made on the death certificate!

Gamache Family Archives

Oliver, Sr. and Oliver, Jr. (unknown date)

Gamache Family Archives

Oliver, Sr. and unknown woman with Gamache services coach

Chapter 13

Joseph Lee Gamache (1881 – 1928) was the author's grandfather. He died before the author's birth. Only one grandmother **Theresa Daisy Rohtert** (1884 – 1973) was known. Daisy outlived my father and mother. She was a small boned woman, not necessarily frail, that crocheted, made rugs out of her son's ties, and visited each Christmas. She lived in an apartment house on Texas Avenue in St. Louis; her sister Annie lived across the hall. The other apartment of the top floor belonged to Mrs. Day. Everybody got along so well the front doors were always open. After a fire consumed most of it, long after Daisy and Annie passed on, the apartment building was demolished. Regretfully, many questions about the family were not asked when she was alive.

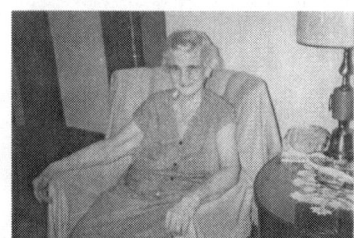

Gamache Family Archives

Theresa Daisy Gamache

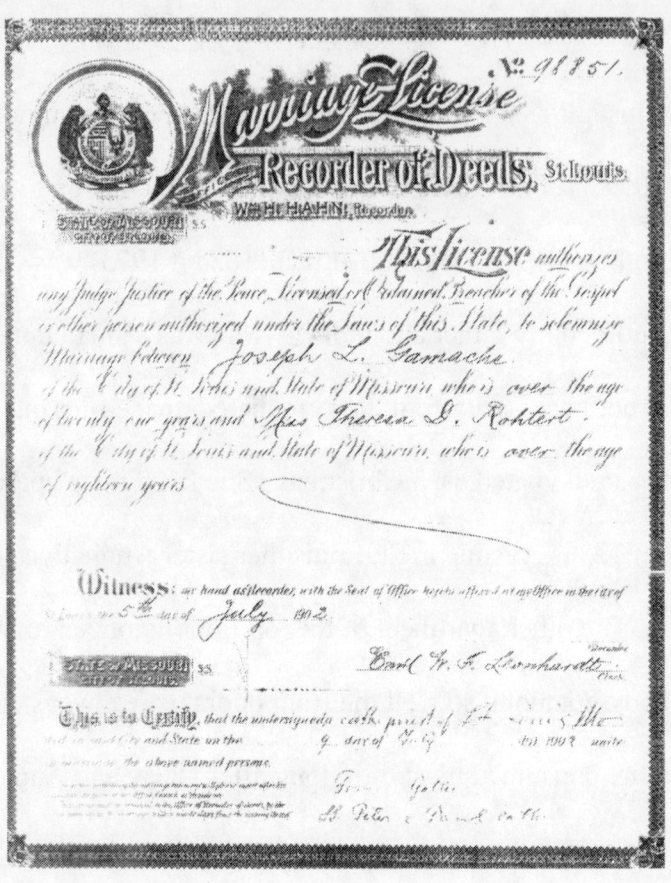

Gamache Family Archives

Joseph Lee and Theresa Daisy Marriage Certificate

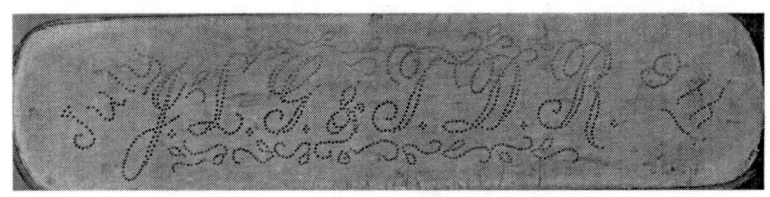

Gamache Family Archives

A Clothes Brush Wedding Present

Joseph Lee (called Lee by his family and friends) and Theresa on July 9, 1902. The clothes brush was given as a wedding present. The numerals "1902" are formed by the bristles on the brush.

Gamache Family Archives

Joseph Lee Gamache

Joseph Lee was a fireman, President of Gamache Motor Car Company, and an amateur musician who played the drums as well as other instruments. What was amazing is that he accomplished these skills without the ability to read or write, although he was able to sign his name. In the 1920's and 1930's he partnered with his son, who was Vice President and Secretary (at age 22!), to run Gamache Motor Car Company in St. Louis. His wife Daisy, my grandmother, was Treasurer. The Gamache Motor Car Company sold the Moon automobile exclusively. The Moon, manufactured in St. Louis, was a luxury car selling at $3,500 to $4,500 at a time when Ford was selling his car for under a $1,000. The Moon plant went out of business in 1936 after manufacturing 450,000 automobiles. Presently, less than 100 Moon's survive. Since Joseph Lee (Lee to his friends and family) could neither read nor write, he would calculate the price of an automobile in his head, add taxes, service charges, etc. and write down a figure. Verified by adding machine, he always was right on the mark! As drummer he occasionally would play gigs with his pianist son.

Gamache Family Archives

Gamache Motor Car Company, St. Louis

The Gamache Motor Car Company had several addresses in St. Louis. The picture above the address is "6828", probably on

Gravois but the 1925 Polk-Gould Business Directory for St. Louis listed the company as 5617 Gravois Avenue with a phone number of "Riverside 2980".

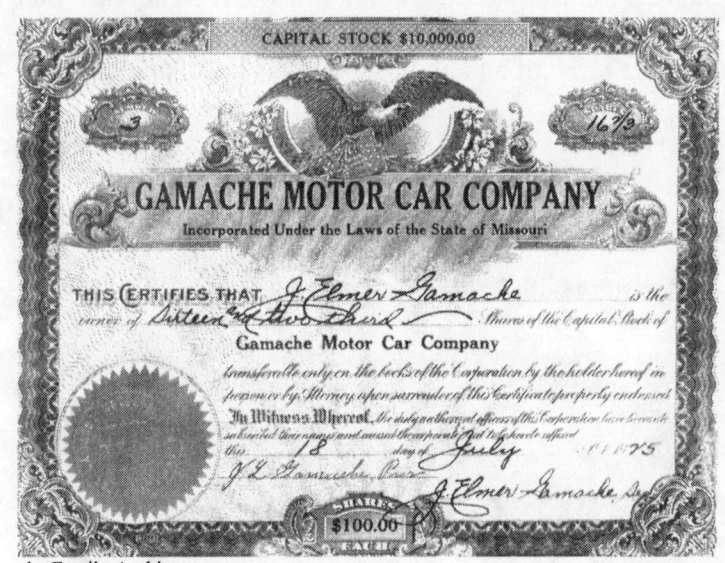

Gamache Family Archives

Stock Certificate in Gamache Motor Car Company

Gamache Family Archives

1929 Moon Automobile

Joseph and Daisy had two children: my father **Joseph Elmer** (1903 – 1971); and Viola (1906 – 1980). Both Joseph Lee and Daisy are buried in St. Peter and Paul Cemetery in St. Louis.

Gamache Family Archives

Joseph Lee and Theresa Daisy Gamache

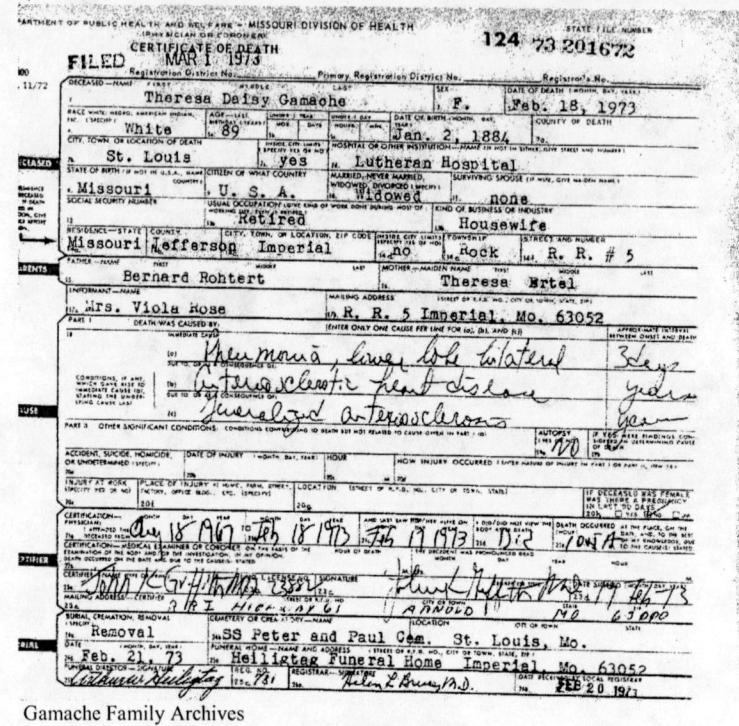

Gamache Family Archives

Theresa Daisy Gamache's Death Certificate

Gamache Family Archives

Joseph Lee Gamache's Death Certificate

Chapter 14

Joseph Elmer, who was called J. Elmer most of his adult life was born at home September 20, 1903, and, according to the birth records, Daisy's sister Annie witnessed the birth. He was born less than three months before the Wright brothers flew their airplane in Kitty Hawk, December 17, 1903, and lived to see man on the moon! He married **May Louise Kolb** (1905 – 1972) on June 24, 1925. Her mother, Josephine, had suffered a disabling stroke years before and May was caring for her and continued caring for her until she died on January 16, 1937. Josephine did not live with my parents but lived in her own home miles away from the newlyweds. Each day my mother would walk and take a trolley to her mother's. She would feed, bath her, and cook all the day's food. At night her father would attend Josephine's needs. My maternal grandparent, Richard Kolb, developed a cyst on his forehead. He was so worried about the operation he had a heart attack and died. His wife died nine months later. The family kept his death a secret until shortly before Josephine's death. She kept asking for Richard, but she was so sick herself from the stroke that she barely remembered that long ago he stopped coming to see her.

J. Elmer and May are buried in Calvary Cemetery, Ottumwa, Iowa.

Gamache Family Archives

J. Elmer and May Gamache

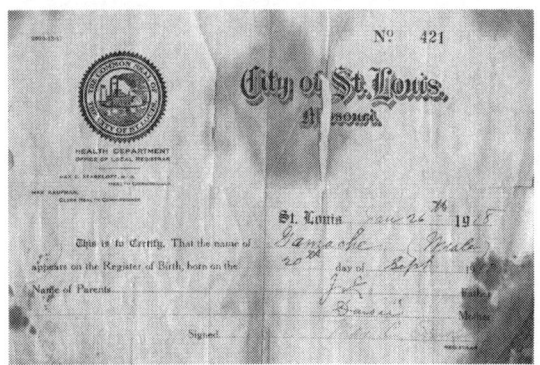

Gamache Family Archives

Joseph Elmer Gamache's Birth Certificate

Gamache Family Archives

May Louise Kolb's Birth Certificate

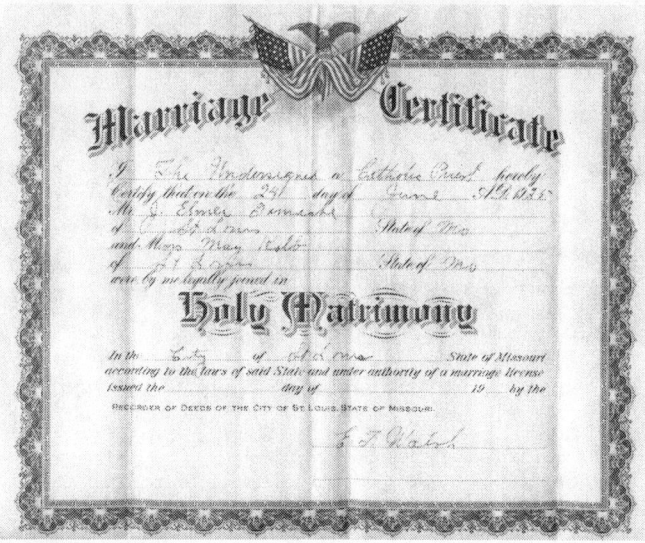

Gamache Family Archives

J. Elmer and May's Marriage Certificate

Gamache Family Archives

J. Elmer Gamache's Death Certificate

126

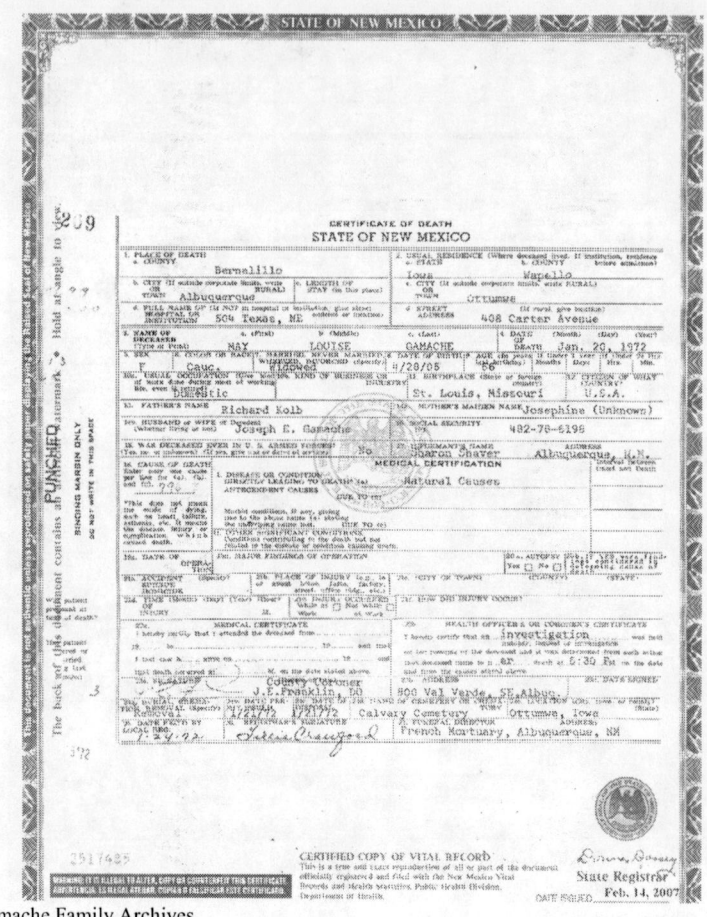

Gamache Family Archives

May Louise Gamache's Death Certificate

My father died in Ottumwa Hospital after battling the effects of alcoholism for many years. My mother died while visiting my twin sister in Albuquerque. One afternoon before dinner she was taking a nap and never woke up. Neither parent talked much about genealogy. I now know more about my genealogy than when my parents were alive while one grandparent was still living.

Lineage on the maternal side is quite straightforward. The parents of May were Richard F. Kolb and Josephine Anna (Bayer) Kolb. They had five children: Theodore, Hilda, Walter (called Mike), May, and Louise. Josephine's parents were Louis Bayer and Anna Heffner, both born in Germany. Richard's parents were Albert and Christine; both were born in Saxony. They had three children, all born in St. Louis: Charles, Richard, and David. May's parents and grandparents died before I was born. U. S. Census data shows the parents lived in St. Louis. The grandparents also immigrated to St. Louis from Germany and Saxony but delineated no town so it would be difficult to trace further.

Gamache Family Archives

Richard Kolb's Death Certificate

Gamache Family Archives

Josephine Kolb's Death Certificate

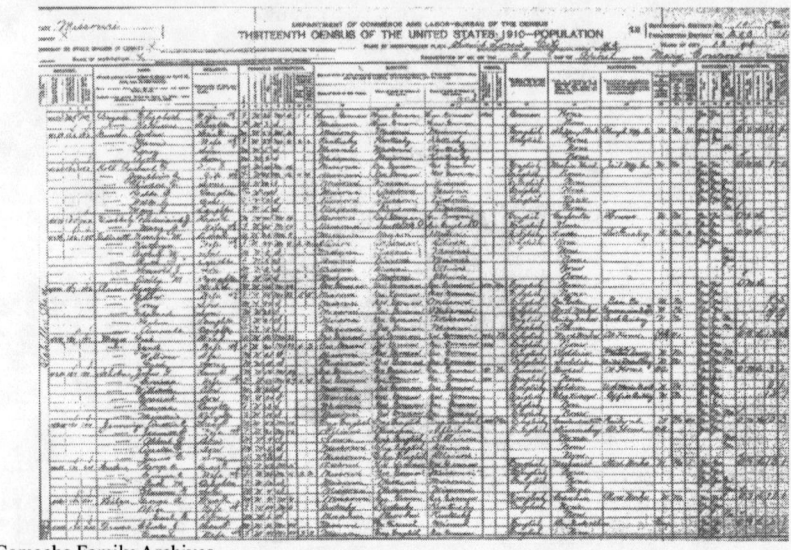

Gamache Family Archives

1910 Federal Census showing Richard Kolb's household

Gamache Family Archives

1870 Federal Census showing Albert Kolb's household

My mother's younger sister was Louise. The two of them got into an argument and did not talk for 29 years even though they lived only a block from each other. They finally meet at a common friends funeral, exchanged greetings and never spoke again. One other story I remember Mom telling was of an uncle who had a sister who never married. The sister was quite progressive and when electricity became available in her neighborhood signed up to place one bulb in the kitchen. The kitchen had 14 foot walls and after awhile the bulb burned out. The sister, through a network of common friends, relayed a message to the brother to come and replace the bulb. The brother, receiving the message, had to walk several miles, take a streetcar, and than walk several miles again before arriving at the sister's house. Up on the ladder and about to remove the bulb, the brother heard the sister cry, "Wait a minute!". Under the sink she withdrew a large wash pan and lifted up to the brother. "What the hell is this for?", he asked. "To catch the juice!" Evidently, the sister heard the word "juice" as a synonym for "electricity" and she really believed there was juice that came pouring out of the open socket.

J. Elmer, in addition to running Gamache Motors, was a musician who had started piano lessons at age 5. By the time he was a young man, it was reported he was making $1,000 a week performing for silent movies as well as private gigs with his father. One of the author's high school memories is of his trio playing at the high school prom.

Gamache Family Archives

J. Elmer Gamache

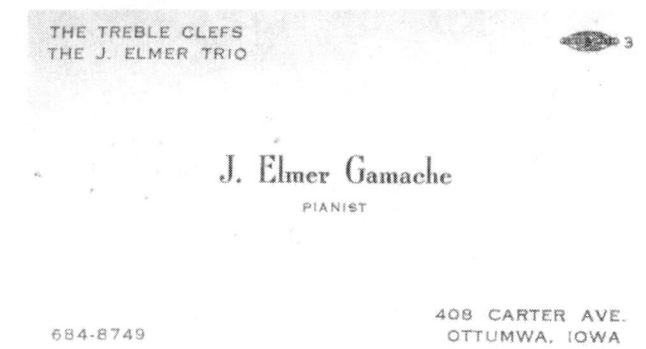

Gamache Family Archives

J. Elmer's Business Card

In the 1930's during the depression, Gamache Motors went out of business and J. Elmer went to work as a salesman for Crunden Martin Manufacturing Company in St. Louis. The company transferred him in 1934 to Des Moines, Iowa, where all of the children, Rynard Andre (1936 -) and the twins Sharon Kay and Gerald Lee (1942 -) were born.

Gamache Family Archives

December 30, 1942 – TWINS!

In 1947, J. Elmer accepted the position of Office Manager at Niemeyer Brothers, a paper wholesale business, in Ottumwa, Iowa where we lived until each child graduated from High School. In 1952 the family purchased a 117-acre farm.

Gamache Family Archives

Farm House, R.F.D. 7, Ottumwa, Iowa

We raised four Black Angus, two horses, chickens and ducks, a dog Fritz, and one pet white rabbit, Snowball. The farm was backbreaking labor and was never a financial success. We sold hogs and beef for less than it cost to feed them. Mom, Sharon and I, supplemented income by selling produce in the summer time. One summer time we were all watching a western on TV and the galloping horses seemed so real. The horses had broken the fence and taken off down the road. The farm was sold around 1966 and Mom and Dad moved to Carter Avenue in town. J. Elmer and May are buried at Calvary Cemetery in Ottumwa right across from the hospital where my Dad died.

Rynard went to college, first at Ames (Iowa State) and than graduated from Iowa State Teachers College in Cedar Falls. He married Mary Theora Wigton June 6, 1959. Both taught in Kenosha, Wisconsin until retirement. Rynard was a Social Studies teacher and Mary taught French and Spanish. They now live in Tucson, Arizona.

Twin sister, Sharon, married Melvin Ray Shaver January 29, 1966. They live in Arnold, Missouri. Sharon retired May 25, 2006 from her position as teacher/teacher-aide. Mel retired after spending 30 years with Defense Mapping Agency and has since retired from his consulting position in September 2007. Sharon and Mel's one child Marsha Ann, married Roger Fields May 21, 1988. Roger is a Captain on the St. Genevieve, Missouri Police Department. Two sons, were born, Blake, August 27, 1991 and Kyle, born June 5, 1994. They both are gifted musicians.

Gerald (Jerry, to every one else except Mother) joined the Iowa National Guard September 1960 at the beginning of my senior year in high school. I attended one semester at State College of Iowa (previously Iowa State Teachers College and now the

University of Northern Iowa) in the spring of 1962. In the summer I moved to Cedar Rapids.

My first wife was Elaine Kaye Hartkemeyer, born February 6, 1942. We were married October 2, 1962 in Detroit. The marriage produced four children: David Anthony, April 20, 1963; Kimberly Kay, April 15, 1965; Erik Terrence, July 28, 1970; and Sarah Michele, November 15, 1971. Kimberly married Kenneth Mark Brantley June 21, 1984 and one child was born, Jessica Erin Brantley on January 14, 1988. Erik married Shanna Strong, born August 25, 1974 on August 12, 1995.

There was a transfer from the Iowa National Guard to U. S. Navy in February 1963, which resulted in five combat tours in Viet Nam between 1966 and 1972. An eventual return to part-time college was made in 1970. In 1972 the Navy transferred me to the Associate Degree Completion Program at Pensacola, Florida, which was completed in 1974. The next Navy assignment was to Jacksonville, Florida where a Bachelor and Master of Arts in Counseling Psychology from University of North Florida were attained. Divorce from Elaine occurred in 1974.

On December 14, 1974, I married Mildred Nichols Koger, Ed. D., educator, psychologist, voice-teacher, and musician who believed in me. I hope I have lived up to her expectations. You are the wind beneath my wings. Prior to retirement from the Navy, I was enrolled in the Industrial-Organizational psychology program and the Ph. D. was awarded 1986 by Old Dominion University.

In 1987, one year after accepting a civil servant position working for the U. S. Army Safety Center, Fort Rucker, Alabama, I suffered a massive stroke. Retirement from civil service with a disability occurred in 1989.

Radiation research had been an endeavor during the graduate years at Old Dominion University. There was involvement with a U. S. Army research grant, which studied soldier competence when exposed to ionizing radiation. In 1992, a letter written to the Editor of the Human Factors Bulletin led to the possibility of researching the Chernobyl accident and studying the physical and cognitive effects of ionizing radiation on the population. Though still disabled, my functioning had much improved. The Defense Nuclear Agency funded a three-month exploratory trip to Ukraine. As Project Director, the trip turned into a ten-year international project with both Ukrainian and American scientists. It was the first research in the world to combine physical and cognitive decrements in performance as a result of exposure to ionizing radiation. The results are published in the Archives of Clinical Neuropsychology, Volume 20, (2005), pages 81 – 93.

Subsequently, the author received the 2005 Outstanding Alumni award from Old Dominion. The Nelson Butters award in 2006 was received for research contributions to clinical Neuropsychology. The International Biographical Centre in Cambridge, England now lists Dr. Gamache as one of the top 2000 scientists of the 20th century. However, the most satisfying accomplishment is the writing of this book.

Endnotes

According to Lisette Gamache, our family has a long history in France for at least a thousand years. Several Counts, Marquis, Lords, and Knights, churchmen and scholars are among those who can lay claim to the Gamache name. In 1377, Billard de Gamache was a knight in the company of Guy de la Rocheguyon. From 1583 to 1610, Antoine Gamache was Dean of Notre Dame church in Mantes-la-Jolie. In the county of Picardy, in the province of Normandy, there are three villages, collectively called Gamaches.

Gamache Family Archives

Mantes-la-Jolie is west of Paris and the villages of Gamaches is directly north along the Bresle River

For over 800 years noblemen, who derived their authority by the King, have ruled the villages of Gamache. They built castles, erected mansions, collected taxes, and protected their fiefdoms. Most were military men who gained their title through service to the King. Some were more than illustrious, for example Joachim Rouhault de Gamaches was Marshall of France, the highest military honor and Philip Gamaches, a doctor of theology who taught at the Sorbonne in Paris. In 1634 his commentary on the writings of St. Thomas Aquinas was published.

Today, in France, there still exist castles, chateaus, and stately homes that once belonged to the family. In 1590 construction began on the Gamache Chateau and was completed in 1650 two years before our arrival in Québec.

Gamache Family Archive

Gamache Chateau near Paris

Finally, all titles were discontinued after the rein of Napoleon III, but in proud families, titles are connections with the past. The Count of Paris, Henri Bourbon, is still referred to as the "pretender to the throne of France." One only has to look at Spain after Franco, when the monarchy was restored, to believe in miracles.

It has been enjoyable researching this book. There is a thrill you get when you discover, especially on the Internet, a document related to your family. This book could not have been written 20 years ago. Information, contained on the Internet, used to lie in dusty file cabinets, or boxes buried in some government warehouse and were largely inaccessible. Today, almost anybody can find census reports, 19th century probate cases, and cemetery records.

My advice to anyone wanting to pursue genealogy is to acquire birth, death, and marriage certificates in order to establish connections between one generation and the next. Most states did not require these vital statistics to be recorded until well into the 20th century. Many times there are multiple sites where States store records, and no site to advise you as to the correct source of the record you want!

Finally, you should interview, interview, interview family members, mothers, father, grandparents, and, if you are fortunate enough, great grandparents to talk about their lives. Use a tape recorder! Nothing is stronger than a person's own recollections of the life lived. Where one worked, lived, and went on vacation, would be so interesting. These stories would tell a story so much richer than mere census reports, birth certificates, and death certificates. Each time I held a death certificate I was reminded of the opportunities missed to question people and regretted not doing so.

An early researcher in St. Louis county history suggested Jean Baptiste D'Gamache was born in Paris in 1665 and at the age of 17 joined LaSalle when he explored the Mississippi in 1682. In an argument with Henri de Tonti, Jean Baptiste was struck in the face by Tonti's iron prosthesis and scarred. Gamache died in 1769 at the age of 104. Unfortunately, this story is a myth. There was no Jean-Baptiste born in 1665. As stated in this book, Alphonse Tonty, the brother of Henri, was Commandant of Fort Detroit. The only connection with the Gamache family was Marie de Tonty, Alphonse's daughter, and Henri's niece, had a daughter Charlotte who married Jean-Baptiste (Bapette) Gamache in St. Louis 1767 (see Page 56).

The St. Louis Genealogical Society has instituted a section called "First Families". The first Families are divided into three groups: Founding Families (1765 – 1804); Pioneer Families (1805 – 1821); and Immigrant Families (1822 – 1865). The Gamache family is proud of our designation as one of the Founding Families.

Gamache Family Archive

First Families of St. Louis Certificate

Gamache Family Archives

Sandra Recker, Chair, First Families Committee

Joining your local genealogical society or group, supporting their efforts by attending meetings and presentations, and sharing information concerning your research strengthens the genealogical movement in the United States. For more information on the St. Louis Genealogical Society contact www.stlgs.org. To learn more about genealogy contact www.ancestory.com or www.genealogy.com.

Appendix A

The Genealogy of Gerald Lee Gamache

(Bold print means a direct relationship)

Parents

Father: **Joseph Elmer Gamache** (1903 - 1971)
Mother: m: (1925) **May Louise Kolb** (1905 – 1972)

Children:

Rynard Andre Gamache (1936 -)
  m: (1959) Mary Theora Wigton (1938 -)
***Sharon Kay Gamache** (1942 -)
  m: (1966) Melvin Ray Shaver (1943 -)
    c: **Marsha Ann Shaver** (1966 -)
      m: (1988) Roger Wayne Fields (1963 -)
        c: **Blake Darden Fields** (1991-)
        c: **Kyle Wayne Fields** (1994 -)
*Gerald Lee Gamache (1942 -)
  m: (1962) Elaine Kay Hartkemeyer (1942 -)
    c: **David Anthony Gamache** (1963 -)
    Kimberly Kaye Gamache (1965 -)
     m: (1984) Kenneth Mark Brantley (1960 – 2004)
       c: **Jessica Erin Brantley** (1988 -)
    Erik Terrence Gamache (1970 –)
     m: (1995) Shanna Marie Strong (1974 -)
    Sarah Michele Gamache (1971 -)
  m: (1974) Mildred Nichols Koger (1928 -)
* Twins

Grandparents

Grandfather: Joseph Lee Gamache (1881-1928)
Grandmother: m: (1902) **Theresa Daisy Rohtert** (1884 – 1973)

Children:

Joseph Elmer Gamache (1903-1971)
Viola Gamache (1908 – 1980)
 m: Maurice McGahan
 m: Kenneth Rose

Great Grandparents

Great-grandfather: Oliver **L. Gamache, Sr.** (1857-1921)
Great-grandmother: m: (1880) **Medora Tesson** (1861 – 1911)

Children:

Cecelia Gamache (1886 - ?)
 m: George Brown
Oliver L. Gamache, Jr. (1894 – 1970)
 m: (1912) Bertha Scharpenburg (1892 – 1980)
Joseph Lee Gamache (1881-1928)

Great Great Grandparents

Great-great grandfather: **Pierre (Peter) Gamache** (1825 - 1900)
Great-great grandmother: m: (1844) (1) **Josephine Pigeon**   (? – before 1862):
                m: (1862) (2) Mary Dillon   (1833 – 1910)

Children: (from Josephine Pigeon)

Jean-Baptiste Gamache (1848 - ?)
  m: Elaine O'Donnell
Peter Gamache (? - ?)
  m: Mary Buscharde
Brigit Gamache (1850 – 1850)
Alexander Gamache (1853 - ?)
  m: Susan Morgan
Andrew Gamache (1859 - ?)
  m: Roselina Kaiser
Oliver L. Gamache (1857- 1921)

Children: (from Mary Dillon)

Francis Gamache (1863 - ?)
  m: (1) Charles Vail
  m: (2) Samuel Champaige
Edward George Gamache (1866 – 1939)
  m: Marguerite Ziefle (? – 1935)
Mary Josephine Gamache (1869 – 1926)
  m: (1888) (1) Harry Sylvester Sharpley (1855 – 1914)
  m: (2) Jack Norris
Marguerite Gamache (1870 - ?)
Bridellia Gamache (1872 - ?)
  m: (1) Joseph Roy
  m: (2) John Hallron
Magdaline Gamache (1874 - 1951)
  m: Herman Merten
Tobias Julian Gamache (1875 – 1931)
  m: (1908) Auguta Zweiger (1888 – 1976)
Anna Gamache (1877 - ?)
  m: John Watkins

Great Great Great Grandparents

Great-great-great grandfather: **Jean-Baptiste Gamache** (1790-1846)
Wife: m: (1813) Brigette Riviere (1793 – 1823)

Children:

Jean-Baptiste Gamache (1815 – died in infancy)
Joseph Gamache (1818 – died in infancy)
Brigette Gamache (1820 - ?)
Octavia Gamache (1823 - ?)

Great-great-great grandmother: m: (1827 after civil 1824) **Françoise (Francis) Vien** (1803 - ?)

Children:

Pierre (Peter) Gamache (1825-1900)
*Marguerite Gamache (1828 - ?)
  m: William Proveau, Sr.
Francis Gamache (1831 infant death)
Emilie Gamache (1832 infant death)
Françoise Gamache (1834 - ?)
  m: Auguste Grenon
Maria (Marie) Gamache (1836 - ?)
  m: Peter Delor
Edward Gamache (1838 - ?)
  m: Marie Grenon
*Eliza Gamache (1840 - ?)
  m: William Proveau, Sr.
* Eliza married the widower (William Proveau, Sr.) of her sister Marguerite

Fourth Great Grandparents

Fourth great grandfather: **Jean-Baptiste Gamache** (1768 – 1839)
Fourth great grandmother: m: (1787) **Catherine Marguerite Constant**
(1771 – 1833)

Children:

Jean-Baptiste Gamache (1789-1846)
Gabriel Gamache (1791 – 1831)
 m: Emily Solomon (1802 – 1833)
   m: Jean Boucher (after the death of Gabriel)
Euphrosine Gamache (1794 - ?)
 m: John E. Leitensdorfer (1772 – 1845)
Joseph Gamache (1796 – 1872)
 m: (1819) Marguerite Boucher
Nicolas Gamache (1800 - ?)
 m: Sophia Boucher
   m: Louis Courtois (after the death of Nicolas)
Catherine Gamache (1805 - ?)
 m: (1833) Gregoire Solomon (after civil 1828)
 m: (1838) Richard Redis Boucher (after civil 1835)
Louis David Gamache (1808 – 1897)
 m: Elizabeth (Diamond) Dahmen (1813 – 1889)

Fifth Great Grandparents

Fifth great grandfather: **Jean-Baptiste Gamache** (1734-1805)
Fifth great grandmother: m: (1767) **Marie-Charlotte D'Amours**
 de Leuvieres (1746 – 1781)

Children:

Jean-Baptiste Gamache (1768 - 1839)
Augustin Gamache (1774 – 1830)
  m: (1794) Genevieve Courtois
Marie Theresa Gamache (June 8, 1776 – August 8, 1776)
Louis Gamache (1778 - ?)
Francois Xavier Gamache (1780 – 1784)

Sixth Great Grandparents

Sixth great grandfather: **Jean-Baptiste Gamache** (1704 - 1748)
Sixth great grandmother: m: (1730) **Elizabeth Bazin** (1710 - ?)

Children:

Jeanne Elizabeth Gamache (1733 - ?)
  m: (1756) Joseph-Basile Gagné
Jean-Baptiste Gamache (1734- 1805)
Joseph Marie Gamache (1736 - ?)
  m: (1757) Marie-Elizabeth Fournier (1731 - ?) veuve Isaac Treilly
    c: Marie-Victoire (1758 - ?)
    c: Louis (1759 - ?)
Nicolas Gamache (1737 - ?)
Augustin Gamache (1739 – 1744)
Jean Gamache (1742 - ?)
Marie Claire Gamache (1744 - ?)
Marie-Madeline Gamache (1746 - ?)

Seventh Great Grandparents

Seventh great grandfather: **Louis Gamache** (1678-1745)
Seventh great grandmother: m: (1702) **Angelique Miville-Deschenes**
(1683 – 1745)
Children:

Louis Gamache (1703 - 1756)
  m: (1732) Madeleine Tibaut (1713 - ?)
    c: Marie-Louise (1734 - ?)
      m: (1757) Joseph Morneau
    c: Still-born (April 13, 1735)
    c: Marie-Madeleine (1736 - ?)
      m: (1758) Pierre Bernier
    c: Marie-Elisabeth (1737 - ?)
      m: (1761) Louis Fortin
    c: Louis-Marie (1739 - ?)
      m: (1763) Marie-Charlotte Dupont (1739 - ?)
    c: Félix ((1740 - ?)
    c: Jean-François (1742 - ?)
      m: (1767) Marie-Madeleine Horesteille (1746 - ?)
    c: Marie-Thérèse (1743 - ?)
    c: Prosper-Marie (Jun 18 – Aug 3, 1746)
    c: Prosper (Jan 28 – Apr 3, 1748)
    c: Marie-Geneviève (1750 - ?)
    c: Joseph-Marie (1753 - ?)
    c: Jean-Baptiste (1754 - ?)+
Jean-Baptiste Gamache (1704 - 1748)
Geneviève Elizabeth Gamache (1705 - ?)
 m: (1734) Ambroise Fournier
Joseph Gamache (1707 – 1733)
Francois Gamache (1709 – 1789)
  m: (1734) Marie Lemieux (1706 - ?) veuve de Jean Gosselin
    c: Marie-Françoise (1735 – 1770)
      m: (1753) François Baron
    c: Philippe-Augustin (1736 - ?)
    c: Marie (? - ?)
      m: (1760) Jean-Baptiste Pilon
      m: (1769) Nicolas Langlois
    c: Antoine (1738 - ?)
      m: (1771) Marie-Anne Loriot
        c: Marie-Anne (1772 - ?)
        c: François-Xavier (1774 - ?)
        c: Marie-Thérèse (Mar 13 – Aug 7, 1782)
    c: Nicolas-François (1740 – 1795)
      m: (1769) Marie-Reine Croteau (? – 1772)

    c: Nicolas (1770 – 1772)
  m: (1775) Marie-Charlotte Truchon (1732 - ?) veuve Pierre Forget
Marie Marthe Gamache (1710 - ?)
  m: (1754) Jean Hilaire Brideau
Ursule Marie Gamache (1712 - 1738)
  m: (1734) Francois Guimont
Madeline Gamache (1714 - 1773)
  m: (1751) Jacques Joncas
Augustin Gamache (1715 - 1739)
Pierre Gamache (1716 - ?)
Ignace Felix Gamache (1718 – 1770)
Michel Arsène Gamache (1721 – 1776)
  m: (1742) Françoise Fournier (1721 – 1762)
    c: Marie-Geneviève (1746 - ?)
    c: Simon (1747 - ?)
    c: Marie-Louise (Feb 16 – Jul 10, 1749)
    c: Marguerite-Ursule (1750 - ?)
    c: Still-born (1751)
    c: Michel (? - ?)
      m: (1775) Marie-Reine Différé
    c: Françoise-Elisabeth (1754 - ?)
    c: Marie-Catherine (1756 - ?)
      m: (1780) Joseph Terrien
    c: Louis-Prosper (1757 - ?)
    c: Still-born (1760)

Eighth Great Grandparents

Eighth great grandfather: **Nicolas Lamarre Gamache** (1639-1699)
Eighth great grandmother: m: (1676) **Elizabeth Ursule Cloutier**
(1660 – 1699)

Children:

Louis Gamache (1678-1745)
Elizabeth Isabelle Gamache (1679 - 1750)
  m: (1709) Pierre Richard (1647 – 1719)
Nicolas Gamache III (1680 – 1734)
  m: (1705) Marie Guyon (1687 - ?)
    c: Geneviève (1705 – ?)
      m: (1731) François-Xavier Caron
    c: Nicolas (1707 – ?)
    c: Augustin (1708 - ?)
    c: Ignace (1710 – ?)
    c: Marie (1712 – 1739)
      m: (1737) Joseph Bélanger
    c: Joachim (1714 – ?)
      m: (1741) Scholastique Tibaut
        c: Joachim (1743 - ?)
          m: (1770) Geneviève Chouinard
            c: Louis-André (1771 – 1773)
            c: Marie-Geneviève (1773 - ?)
            c: Marie-Anne (1776 - ?)
        c: Marie-Judith (1749 – 1750)
        c: Marie-Charlotte (1749 - ?)
        c: Scholastique (1751 - ?)
        c: André (? - ?)
          m: (1772) Marie-Julienne Pelletier
            c: Marie-Françoise (1773 - ?)
            c: André (1774 - ?)
            c: Marie-Charlotte (1775 - ?)
        c: Marie-Geneviève (1755 - ?)
        c: Simon-Alexandre (1757 - ?)
          m: (1781) Ursule Joncas (1755 - ?)
        c: Marie-Joseph (1760 - ?)
    c: Marguerite (1715 - 1737)
      m: (1734) Louis Caron
    c: Elizabeth (1719 - ?)
      m: (1737) François Chalifour
    c: Alexis-Isidore (1721 - ?)
      m: (1748) Hélène Chalifour (1722 - ?) veuve Pierre-Bernard   Auclair
        c: Nicolas (1750 - ?)

        c: Marie-Hélène (1754 - ?)
        c: François (1757 - ?)
        c: Julian (1761 - ?)
    c: Marie-Marthe (1724 - ?)
        m: (1743) Jean Boucher
Jean-Baptiste Gamache (1682 – 1750)
  m: (1712) Agathe Richard (1689 – 1712)
    c: Jean (Nov 23, 1712 – Jan 27, 1713)
  m: (1713) Louise Caron (1692 - ?)
Ignace Gamache (1683 - ?)
Augustin Gamache (1686 – 1714)
  m: (1711) Marguerite Guyon (1690 – 1712)
    c: Augustine (Sept 9 – Nov 7, 1712)
  m: (1713) Louise Caron
    c: Augustin and Nicolas (Aug 20 – Nov 15, 1714)
    c: Louise (1716 - ?)
        m: (1734) Louis Lemieux
Anne Gamache (1690 - 1748)
  m: (1713) Jean-Baptiste Richard
Genevieve Gamache (1692 - 1736)
  m: (1711) Joseph Hudon
  m: (1713) Jean Gagnon
Marie Gamache (1694 - 1759)
  m: (1722) Louis Dion
Pierre Gamache (1698 - 1757)
  m: (?) Marie ----------
    c: Pierre (? - ?)
        m: (1744) Marie-Marguerite Gagné
            c: Marie-Barbe (Feb 3 – Feb 24, 1746)
            c: Marie-Madeleine (1747 - ?)
            c: Henri (1749 - ?)
                m: (1768) Thérèse Côté (1749 - ?)
                    c: Henri (1774 - ?)
            c: Marie-Thérèse (Jan 24 – Mar 23, 1751)
            c: Marie-Louise (May 21 Jun 18, 1752)
            c: Félicité-Euphronsine (1754 – 1755)
            c: Félix-Roch (Jan 17 – 21, 1756)
            c: Marie-Pétronille (1757 - ?)
  m: (1734) Genevieve Belanger (1710 - ?)
    c: Geneviève (1735 - ?)
    c: Marie-Rose (1737 - ?)
        m: (1763) Jean-Baptiste Fournier
    c: Pierre (1739 - ?)
    c: Paschal (1740 – 1741)
    c: Lazare (1744 - ?)
    c: Marguerite (1746 - ?)

c: Aubin (1748 - ?)
c: Marie-Anne (1749 - ?)
c: Jérôme (1753 - ?)
   m: (1777) Véronique Simard (1755 - ?)
c: Augustin-Georges (1757 - ?)

Ninth Great Grandparents

Ninth great grandfather: **Nicolas Gamache** (1595-1676)
          m: (1620) Michele Potel (? - ?)

Children:

Jacques Gamache (1621 -1681)

Ninth great grandmother: m: (1629) **Jacqueline Jeanne Cadotte**
          (1611 – ?)

Children:

Genevieve Gamache (1636 – 1709)
  m: (1652) Julien Bellefaine Fortin (1630 - 1687)
Nicolas Lamarre Gamache (1639-1699)

Tenth Great Grandparents

Tenth great grandfather: **Guillaume Lamarre Gamache** (1565 - ?)
Tenth great grandmother: **Renee Huan** (1575 - ?)

Children:

Nicolas Gamache (1595-1676)

Appendix B

U.S. Supreme Court

STROTHER v. LUCAS, 31 U.S. 763 (1832)

31 U.S. 763 (Pet.)

DANIEL F. STROTHER, PLAINTIFF IN ERROR
v.
JOHN B. C. LUCAS, DEFENDANT IN ERROR.

January Term, 1832

ERROR to the district court of the United States for the district of Missouri.

This was an action of ejectment in the district court of Missouri, brought by Daniel F. Strother of Kentucky, against John B. C. Lucas of Missouri, to recover a tract of land, particularly described in the declaration, containing eighty arpens, adjoining the city of St Louis. The defendant pleaded the general issue, and the cause was tried at the September term 1830, when there was a verdict for the defendant, and judgment rendered thereon; to reverse which, this writ of error is prosecuted. The record contains a bill of exceptions, which sets out at large all the testimony given at the trial, and the decisions of the court, which were excepted to.

Page 31 U.S. 763, 764

The premises in dispute consist of two common field lots, of one by forty arpens each. The common field of St Louis (of which the premises in question are a part) is a large tract of land lying immediately west of the former boundary of the town of St. Louis, and extending for some distance north and south of it. The lots are parallelograms, of one or more arpens in front, and extending westward to the uniform depth of forty arpens. The common field was separated from the town and town lots, by a fence extending the whole length of the eastern front; there were no division fences, though the lots were held and cultivated separately, and each proprietor was bound to keep up the fence in front of his lot. The witnesses, when speaking of these lots, use the term one arpen, two arpens , &c., meaning always the front of the lot spoken of, and the depth must be understood to be forty arpens: thus a lot of one by forty arpens, is called one arpen, &c.

The facts of this cause are these: some time in the year 1772, Don Manuel Duralde surveyed, and laid off into lots, the common field of St Louis. It does not appear, however, that he was an official surveyor, nor does any authority for the survey appear. Among the lots laid off were the two mentioned in the plaintiff's declaration. One of these appear to have been surveyed for Joseph Gamache and the other for Rene Kiercereau. These surveys are shown by two documents set forth in the bill of exceptions, as extracts from the Livre terrien, purporting to be a registry of the returns made by Duralde. In the margin of the registry of the survey for Kiercereau, are these words: '1798, St Cir, I arpen' and on the margin of the registry of the return of Gamache's survey, these words are found: '1793, St Cir, I arpen; and a memorandum in French, which rendered into English is as follows: 'the name of said Gamache is Baptiste instead of Joseph.' There was also some other evidence given at the trial to establish the fact, that the person for whom the survey was made was not Joseph, but Baptiste or John Baptiste Gamache; the lots, thus surveyed, adjoined each other, that of Gamache being on the north and Kiercereau's on the south; the northern lot was bounded on the north by a lot of Bissonet, alias Bijou, and the southern on the south by a lot of Bequette.

On the 9th January 1773, John Baptiste Gamache, by deed of exchange, conveyed to Louis Chancillier, the northern half

of the northern lot; and on the 6th of April 1781, a deed was executed by one Marie Reneux Robillar, purporting to convey to Louis Chancillier, the southern, or Kiercereau's lot. In the body of this deed, Rene Kiercereau is stated to be a subscribing witness, and there is a signature to the deed as such, alleged to be his. There is also some evidence to show that the whole name of the grantor was not written by herself; both these deeds were, however, admitted as evidence. Chancillier cultivated a part of the two lots until his death, which happened in 1785: that is to say, he cultivated the whole front of the southern lot, and the southern half of the northern lot, to the extent of a few arpens in depth. On the 8th of June 1785, after the death of Chancillier an inventory of his estate was taken, and among the items is found one arpen and a half of land in the common fields, which was admitted to have been regularly sold to, and all the title which Chancillier had vested in, Madam Chancillier the widow. It does not appear that any part of the land in question was ever occupied, possessed or cultivated after the death of Chancillier, by any body claiming under him. The widow remained about two years at St Louis, when she intermarried with one Beauchamp; and she and her husband removed immediately to St Charles in the same state, and at a distance of about twenty miles from St Louis, where Beauchamp died. The widow, some time after, was married to one Basil Laroque, who died in 1828. The widow of Chancillier, from the time of her marriage with Beauchamp, until the commencement of this suit, resided in St Charles, and it does not appear that she claimed the premises in dispute until about the year 1818, and, it was alleged, not until she was urged to it by others. On the 12th September 1828, she transferred her claim by deed, to George F. Strother, who conveyed to the plaintiff.

Soon after the death of Chancillier, and some time in the year 1785 or 1786, Hyacinth St Cyr was put into the possession of the two lots in question by the syndistrict, the fence in front not having been kept up, and the lots, therefore, considered as abandoned. St Cyr soon after purchased of Gamache and Kiercereau their claims; he continued to cultivate and possess both lots in his own right, from the time of his first entry in 1785 or 1786, and kept up his part of the fence until the

Page 31 U.S. 763, 766

whole common field inclosure was destroyed in 1798 or 1799. In 1801, Auguste Choteau became the purchaser of the two lots, at the public sale, of the effects of St Cyr, who was an insolvent debtor: and in 1810, the two lots were confirmed to Auguste Choteau by the board of commissioners appointed for the adjustment of land claims. Choteau had, previously to the confirmation, conveyed the lots to the defendant, Jean B. C. Lucas, who has been in the uninterrupted possession ever since the year 1808. These are the material facts of the case as they appear by the bill of exceptions.

At the trial, the plaintiff offered sundry depositions to prove the signature of Kiercereau as witness to the deed of Marie Reneux Robillar. These depositions were rejected. It appeared that not one of the witnesses ever saw him write or knew his hand writing; but it having been proved that Kiercereau had been a chantre in the Catholic church at St Louis, the witnesses had examined the register of the interments and marriages, and the name of Kiercereau appearing subscribed to some of the entries as witness, they were asked to deliver their opinion as to the signature on the deed by comparison with the signatures in the registry, not one of which was proved to have been made by Kiercereau, nor did it appear to have been a part of his official duty to sign the register; and it did appear that there were living witnesses who had seen Kiercereau write and knew his signature; one of whom (Pierre Choteau) was actually examined as a witness in the cause.

On the testimony before the jury, the court, on the prayer of the defendant, gave the following instruction to wit:

If the jury find from the evidence, that the two confirmations to Auguste Choteau, given in evidence by the plaintiff in this case, are for the same land, and include all the premises in the declaration mentioned, the plaintiff cannot recover in this action.

The jury found a verdict for the defendant, upon which judgment was entered by the district court. The plaintiff prosecuted this writ of error.

The case was argued by Mr Benton, with whom was also Mr Taney, for the plaintiff in error; and by Mr Wirt for the defendant.

Page 31 U.S. 763, 767

Mr Justice THOMPSON delivered the opinion of the Court.

This case comes up on a writ of error from the district court of Missouri. It was an action of ejectment for two arpens of land in front and forty arpens in depth, in and adjoining the city of St Louis in the state of Missouri.

The material question in the case arises upon an instruction given to the jury upon the prayer of the defendant below, who is the defendant here.

Upon the trial no evidence was given on the part of the defendant, and the plaintiff having closed his case, the defendant moved the court to instruct the jury as follows: 'that if the jury find from the evidence that the two confirmations made by the board of commissioners to Auguste Choteau, given in evidence by the plaintiff in this case, are for the same land, and include all the premises in the declaration mentioned, the plaintiff cannot recover in this action.' Which instruction was given, and the jury found a verdict for the defendant.

In the course of the trial certain depositions were offered in evidence, which, among other things, went to prove the hand writing of Rene Kiercereau, whose name appeared as a witness to one of the deeds which had been admitted in evidence (and who, in the body of the deed, was described as a witness of assistance), by comparing the hand writing of the witness with the hand writing of entries made in a certain register of marriages and interments, alleged to have been made by the witness; of which, however, there was no direct evidence. The depositions, so far as they went to prove the hand writing of the witness to the deed by comparison, were objected to and overruled by the court, to which exception was taken.

It is a general rule, that evidence by comparison of hands is not admissible, where the witness has had no previous knowledge of the hand writing, but is called upon to testify merely from a comparison of hands. There may be cases, where, from the antiquity of the writing, it is impossible for any living witness to swear that he ever saw the party write, comparison of hand writing with documents, known to be in his hand writing, has been admitted. But these are extraordinary instances, arising from the necessity of the case, and which do not apply to the one before the court. For there were living witnesses examined as to the hand writing, and, besides, the

Page 31 U.S. 763, 768

deed was received and read in evidence, and the plaintiff had the full benefit of it. But it is said, the evidence was offered for the purpose of identifying the witness, and to show that he was the original grantee of the forty arpens, and the husband of Marie Reneux Robillar; and being named in the deed as a witness of assistance, it operated by the Spanish and French law as a conveyance of his own title, the same as if he had signed the deed as grantor.

There are two answers to be given to the objection made to the ruling of the judge in the court below, in the view now presented. In the first place, that was not stated as the purpose for which it was offered, nor was it shown that such was the operation of the deed thus witnessed by the Spanish or French law; and these being foreign laws, should have been proved. The court cannot be charged with knowledge of foreign laws. But, in the second place, the record does not show that the judge was called upon to express any opinion with respect to the legal effect and operation of the deed, or that the plaintiff had not the full benefit of its being considered his deed. And, indeed, it would seem from the course of the trial, that it was so considered, or at all events the contrary does not appear from any question presented to the court on the subject.

Two other points have been made and argued here, which do not appear to have been raised in the court below, and which will be very briefly noticed.

It is objected on the part of the defendant that the plaintiff's claim, even from his own showing, is no more than an equitable right, for which an action of ejectment will not lie.

There is in the state of Missouri an act of the legislature regulating the action of ejectment, and enumerating various classes of cases of claims to land, where the action will lie; among which a claim under any French or Spanish grant, warrant, or order of survey, which, prior to the 10th of March 1804, had been surveyed by proper authority under the French or Spanish governments, and recorded according to the customs and usages of the country. Rev. Laws Miss. 343.

This would seem broad enough to embrace the claim now in question, and authorise the right to be tried in an action of ejectment in the state courts. How far the courts of the

Page 31 U.S. 763, 769

United States will adopt such practice, has come under the consideration of this court in several cases, Robinson v. Campbell, 3 Wheat. 212; De la Croix v. Chamberlain, 12 Wheat. 599; and the court has been strongly inclined against sustaining the action upon a mere equitable title, except perhaps where, by the statutes of a state, a title which would otherwise be deemed merely equitable, is recognized as a legal title, or a title which would be valid at law. We do not mean, however, to be understood as expressing any opinion upon this question in the present case. But as the cause has been tried upon the merits, and so argued here, we think best to decide upon the merits, without noticing the objection to the forms of the action.

An objection rather of a novel character has been made on the part of the plaintiff to the confirmation of the title in Choteau, because the defendant was one of the commissioners who confirmed the claim, and had purchased the lots of Choteau, before the confirmation. On reference to the proceedings of the commissioners, the allegation does not appear to be founded in fact: although he was one of the commissioners, he did not sit with them when this claim was confirmed. But it is a little singular that the plaintiff should himself give this confirmation in evidence in support of his own title, and then attempt to impeach it.

The main question in the cause, however, grows out of the instructions given by the court to the jury: and to a right understanding of that question, a brief statement of the case as it stood when the instruction was given becomes necessary.

The plaintiff as the origin of his title gave in evidence two certified copies of entries of surveys from what is called the Livre Terrien. The one, purporting to be an entry of a survey made for Rene Kiercereau of one by forty arpens: the other, a survey purporting to have been made for Joseph Gamache for the same quantity. On the 29th of January 1773, Gamache conveyed to Louis Chancillier one half of the lot surveyed for him, and on the 6th of April 1781, Marie Reneux Robillar (the wife of Rene Kiercereau) conveyed to Louis Chancillier the lot surveyed for him. Chancillier cultivated a part of these lots until his death in 1785; after his death, his widow, Madame Chancillier, became the purchaser of the one and a

Page 31 U.S. 763, 770

half arpens of land, but did not take possession of or cultivate these lots; nor does it appear that she laid claim to them until about the year 1818; and in September 1828 she sold the lots to George F. Strother, who conveyed the same to the plaintiff. Soon after the death of Chancillier, and some time in the year 1785 or 1786, Hyacinth St Cyr was put into possession of the two lots by the syndic of the district, the fence in front not having been kept up; and from the proceedings of the commissioners introduced by the plaintiff himself, it appears that Kiercereau, on the 23d of October 1793, conveyed to St Cyr his claim to the lot surveyed for him, and on the same day Gamache conveyed to St Cyr his claim to the lot surveyed for him. And by the same proceedings, it appears that at a public sale in the year 1801 made of the property of St Cyr, Auguste Chouteau became the purchaser of these lots, and on the 11th of January 1808, he conveyed the same to the defendant. St Cyr, from the time of his first entry on the lots in 1785 or 1786, continued to cultivate and possess them, and keep up his part of the fence until the whole common field inclosure was destroyed about the year 1798; and Chouteau, from the time of his purchase in 1801 until he sold to the defendant, and the defendant from the time of his purchase, have continued to occupy the same to the present time, and in the year 1820 the claim to the two lots was confirmed to Auguste Choteau by the commissioners.

From this statement of the case, according to the plaintiff's own showing, there is a regular deduction of title or claim, from the persons for whom the lots were surveyed to the defendant. But it appears that those persons, Kiercereau and Gamache, sold their claim twice; in the first place to Louis Chancillier, under whom the plaintiff claims; and in the second place to St Cyr, under whom the defendant claims. If these title papers were to be considered independent of the acts of congress and the proceedings of the commissioners, the plaintiff, being prior in point of time, would prevail, so far as depended upon the deduction of a paper title, and independent of the question of possession.

It becomes necessary, therefore, to inquire how far the acts of congress apply to and affect any part of these title papers; keeping in mind that it is all the plaintiff's own evidence; he

Page 31 U.S. 763, 771

having produced the proceedings before the commissioners, is not now at liberty to deny the facts therein stated.

No grant has been shown under which the plaintiff sets up his claim; his title was therefore incomplete, and by the fourth section of the act of 1805 (3 vol. L. U. S. 653), the person claiming the land was bound to deliver to the register of the land office, or recorder of land titles, within the district where the land lies, a notice in writing stating the nature and extent of his claim; and also to deliver to the said register or recorder, for the purpose of being recorded, every grant, order of survey, deed, conveyance or other written evidence of his claim. And the law directs that they shall be recorded by the register or recorder, &c. with a proviso, however, that where the lands are claimed by virtue of a complete French or Spanish grant, it shall not be necessary for the claimant to have any other evidence of his claim recorded, than the original grant or patent, together with the warrant or order of survey and the plat; but all the other conveyances or deeds shall be deposited with the register or recorder, to be laid before the commissioners. And the act then declares that if such person shall neglect to deliver such notice in writing of his claim, or cause to be recorded such written evidence of the same, all his right, so far as the same is derived from the two first sections of the act, shall become void, and forever thereafter barred. If any doubt should arise whether the original right, claimed in this case, comes within the two first sections of the act, that is removed by the act of 1807 (4 vol. L. U. S. 112), which repeals the proviso to the first section of the act of 1805, and the power of the commissioners is enlarged. The fourth section declares that the commissioners shall have full power to decide, according to the laws and the established usages and customs of the French and Spanish governments, upon all claims to land within their respective districts, where the claim is made by any person or persons, or the legal representative of any person or persons who were, on the 20th of December 1803, inhabitants of Louisiana, and for a tract not exceeding the quantity of acres contained in a league square, &c. which decision of the commissioners, when in favour of the claimant, shall be final against the United States. And the time is extended for delivering notices and evidences of

Page 31 U.S. 763, 772

the claim, but declaring that the rights of such persons as shall neglect so doing, shall, so far as they are derived from or founded on any act of congress, ever after be barred and become void, and the evidences of their claims never after admitted as evidence in any court of law whatever. There is no evidence that notice of the claim, now set up, was ever given as required by these laws; or that the deeds from Kiercereau and Gamache to Chancillier were ever delivered to be recorded as required by the law. And Madam Chancillier, having slept upon this claim for so great a length of time, from the year 1785 to 1818, there is every reason to conclude she had abandoned it; and these deeds cannot now, under the provisions of these laws, be received as evidence of any right to be established under the acts of congress. And it must have been understood, upon the trial, that the plaintiff sought to establish his right under these acts of congress, or he would not have produced the confirmation of the commissioners as evidence of his right. But having relied upon it in support of his own claim, he ought not now to be permitted to deny that it was one properly submitted to the commissioners. Had he rested his claim upon a title derived from Chancillier, without the aid of the acts of congress, the evidences of his title would not have been affected by those acts; but the defendant would, in that case, have been fully protected by his length of possession. When, however, a part of the plaintiff's evidence was the proceedings of the commissioners upon this very claim, this court must consider the instruction of the judge as referring only to the effect and operation of the confirmation under the laws in relation to such claims. And in that view of the case the instruction was perfectly correct.

There is, however, some obscurity in the application of the instruction given by the court; but from the evidence set out in the bill of exceptions, we cannot say there was any error. Any the justice and law of the case, growing out of such a length of possession, are so manifestly with the judgment in the court below, if we look at the whole evidences on the record; that we feel disposed to give the most favourable interpretation to the instructions of the court. And we the more readily incline to think the light in which the instruction is here considered was that in which it was understood on the

Page 31 U.S. 763, 773

trial, because the counsel for the plaintiff in error has contended on the argument here, that this confirmation enures to the benefit of the owner of the claim: that the commissioners decide only the abstract right, as against the United States, without regard to the person who sets up the claim. And it is upon this ground only, that the plaintiff would have introduced in evidence the decision of the commissioners which was directly against his own right; he thereby probably expecting to destroy the effect of the adverse possession, and make the possession as well as the confirmation of the commissioners enure to his benefit. But this view of the case cannot be sustained; and the judgment of the court below must be affirmed.

This cause came on to be heard on the transcript of the record from the district court of the United States for the district of Missouri, and was argued by counsel; on consideration whereof, it is adjudged and ordered that the judgment of the said district court in this cause be, and the same is hereby affirmed, with costs.

Appendix C

U.S. Supreme Court

GAMACHE v. PIQUIGNOT, 57 U.S. 451 (1853)

57 U.S. 451 (How.)

LOUIS D. GAMACHE, SAMUEL AND LEONORE GAMACHE, BY GUARDIAN, WILSON PRIMM, LOUIS PRIMM, JOHN CAVENDEN, AND ABBY P. TRUE, PLAINTIFFS IN ERROR,
v.
FRANCOIS X. PIQUIGNOT, AND THE INHABITANTS OF THE TOWN OF CARONDELET.

December Term, 1853

Page 57 U.S. 451, 452

THIS case was brought up from the Supreme Court of Missouri by a writ of error issued under the 25th section of the Judiciary Act.

It was an action in the nature of an ejectment brought by the plaintiffs in error, for the recovery of a tract of land described in the declaration as survey No. 120 of the out lots and common field lots of the village of Carondelet.

The substance of the two acts of Congress of 1812 and 1824 is given in the caption of this report, and need not be repeated.

Upon the trial, the plaintiff offered the three following pieces of evidence, all of which were rejected by the court. There was much other evidence offered both by the plaintiffs and defendants; but as the opinion of this court turned chiefly upon the propriety of this rejection, the other pieces of evidence, and instructions of the court founded thereon, will be omitted. It will be perceived that each one of the three purports to derive its efficary from the certificate of Mr. Conway, in 1839

The plaintiffs then offered in evidence the following certificate of confirmation of the recorder of land titles of Missouri, as follows, to wit: (Indorsed on the outside 'Jno. Bte. Gamache, sen., 6 by 40 arpens, field of Carondelet. Fees $1, paid.') John Baptiste De Gamache, sen., or his legal representatives, claims an out lot, adjoining the village of Carondelet, containing six arpens in front by forty in depth, bounded, northerly, by the common fields; eastwardly, by the Mississippi River (leaving a tow between it and the river); south, by an out lot claimed by the legal representatives of Gabriel Constant, (lalmond,) sen., an[d] west by the land formerly the property of Antoine Riehl.

John Baptiste Maurice Chatillon, being duly sworn, says he knows the land claimed, and that he is about sixty-six years of age, and that he was born in Kaskaskia, and A. D. seventeen hundred and eighty-eight he removed from Ste. Genevieve to Carondelet, where he has resided ever since; that A. D. seventeen hundred and ninety-seven or ninety-eight he was employed by John Baptiste Gamache, sen., to fence in a field which said Gamache had been clearing, and working for about two years within this field lot; and he, this respondent, says, he did fence in about three arpens of this land, and did build a cabin on the same at this time; and this deponent further says that Gamache did cultivate this same field for five or six years until his death;

Page 57 U.S. 451, 453

and this deponent further says he always understood this land was owned by said John Baptiste Gamache.

JOHN BAPTISTE MAURICE his X mark. CHATILLON.

Sworn to before me, July 6th, 1825.

THEODORE HUNT, Recorder L. T.

Translated to witness. J. V. GARNIER.

RECORDER'S OFFICE,

ST. LOUIS, Missouri, 22d January, 1839.

I certify the foregoing within to be truly copied from book No. 2, page 46, of the minutes of the proceedings of the recorder of land titles in the State of Missouri, under the act of Congress of the 26th May, 1824, entitled 'An act supplementary of an act passed on the 13th day of June, 1812,' entitled 'An act making further provisions for settling the claims to land in the territory of Missouri,' all of record in this office, and confirmed by the act of 13th June, 1812, above cited.

F. R. CONWAY,

U. S. Recorder of Land Titles in the State of Missouri.

TO DANIEL DUNKLIN, Esq.,

U. S. Surveyor of Public Lands, St. Louis, Mo.

Together with a certified extract from the registry of certificates from the office of the recorder of land titles as follows, to wit:

Registry of Certificates of confirmation on town lots, out lots, and common field lots, issued by the Recorder of Land Titles.

[]

In whose name issued. Date. Situation. Remarks. Quantity. [] The following claim was ommitted by Mr. Hunt, late recorder, in furnishing the list of claims proven up before him, to wit: John Baptiste de Gamache. 6th July, 1825. Carondelet fields. Bounded north by the common fields, eastwardly by the Missippi, (leaving a tow [path] between it and the river,) south by an out lot claimed by the le- gal representatives of Gabriel Constant, (lalmond,) sen. and westwardly by the land formerly the property of Antoine Rheil.

[]

Page 57 U.S. 451, 454

The above claim entered by me in the book, 12th March, 1839, having this day furnished the surveyor-general with a description thereof.

F. R. CONWAY, Recorder. RECORDER'S OFFICE, ST. LOUIS, January 23d, 1851. The above is correctly copied from the registry on file in this office. ADOLPH RENARD, U. S. Recorder of Land Titles in the State of Missouri.

And also a certified extract from the list of claims proved before the recorder of land titles, under the act of 26th of May, 1824, (in which is contained the Gamache claim to which particular reference was made at this stage of the case,) transmitted by the recorder of land titles to the surveyor-general of the United States in Illinois and Missouri, certified from the office of the surveyor-general as follows, to wit:

(This was a list of cases transmitted by Mr. Hunt to the surveyor-general, as a supplemental report. The cases bear various dates, the last being 12th April, 1830. They were 16 in number. Then came the following, transmitted by Mr. Conway, accompanied by a certificate by him, dated 12th March, 1839, stating that it had been omitted to be furnished by his predecessor, Mr. Hunt.)
No. 17
-Not in list.

John Baptiste de Gamache, senior, or his legal representatives, claim an out lot adjoining the village of Carondelet, containing six arpens in front by forty in depth, bounded northerly by the common, eastwardly by the Mississippi, (leaving a tow between it and the river,) south by an out lot claimed by the legal representatives of

Gabriel Constant, (Lalamand) senior, and west by the land formerly the property of Antoine Rheil.

John Baptiste Maurice Chatillon, being duly sworn, says he knows the land claimed, and that he is about sixty-six years of age, and that he was born in Kaskaskia, and A. D. 1788, he removed from St. Genevieve to Carondelet, where he has resided ever since; that A. D. seventeen hundred ninety-seven or ninety (8) eight he was employed by John Baptiste Gamache, senior, to fence in a field-which said Gamache had been clearing and working in for about two years within this field lot-and he, this deponent, says he did fence about three arpens of this land, and build a cabin on the same, at this time. And this deponent further says, that Gamache did cultivate this same field for five or six years until his death. And this deponent

Page 57 U.S. 451, 455

further says, he always understood this land was owned by said John Baptiste Gamache.

(Signed) JOHN BAPTISTE MAURICE his X mark. CHATILLON. Sworn to before me, July 6th, 1825. (Signed) THEODORE HUNT, Rec'r L. T. Translated to witness by J. V. Garnier.

The plaintiff also offered in evidence a certified extract from Hunt's minutes, containing the entry of Gamache's claim, with a description of the lot; and also the evidence therein recorded, but the court refused to receive it; and also testimony to prove the inhabitation and cultivation of the lot prior to December, 1803, and until his death in 1805. There was also much other evidence which need not be stated in this report.

The defendants offered evidence

1. To show a title under the act of Congress, of 1812, as commons of Carondelet.

2. An adverse possession for twenty years.

3. Rebutting evidence.

After the evidence was closed various instructions were asked for both, by the counsel for plaintiff and defendant, some of each of which were given and some refused by the court, as the verdict was for the defendants, and the case was brought up by the plaintiffs, only those instructions and refusals to which they excepted, will be here stated.

Instructions for plaintiffs refused. 3. The jury are instructed that, as against such a claim and cultivation, or possession, as that mentioned in said second instructions, no adverse user as commons as a ground of title, under the act of Congress of 13th June, 1812, can prevail, unless such user existed in fact by an actual occupation and use as commons of the same ground, visible and continued, notorious, hostile, and exclusive, [and then] only to the extent that such actual occupation and use as commons existed in fact, and to the exclusion of such claim and cultivation, or possession, by Gamache, of the same land as an out lot, or cultivated field lot, of the village, prior to the 20th day of December, 1803; provided the jury also believe, from the evidence, that the tract of land in the declaration described was claimed and inhabited, cultivated or possessed, by John B. Gamache, senior, prior to the 20th day of December, 1803, as an out lot or cultivated field lot of said village, with such a cultivation or possession as that mentioned in the said second instructions for the plaintiffs.

4. If the jury believe, from the evidence, that the claim of the village of Carondelet to commons, prior to the 20th day of December,

Page 57 U.S. 451, 456

1803, was bounded north (in part) [by] the cultivated lands of the village, and that, prior to said date, the lot of land in said declaration described as having been claimed by Gamache was one of the cultivated lands of the village, then there is no conflict of title in this case, and the defendants have shown no title to the land in controversy.

5. The jury are instructed that, on the evidence given in this case, the statute of limitations is no bar to this action, unless they shall believe, from the evidence, that the town of Carondelet, or those holding under said town, have had an adverse possession in fact of the land in controversy in this case by an actual occupation on the ground, visible and continued, notorious, hostile, and exclusive, for at least twenty years next preceding the commencement of this suit.

7. The jury are instructed that the survey No. 120, and the plats and field notes thereof given in evidence by the plaintiffs, are evidence of the true location, extent, and boundary of the out lot of the village of Carondelet, claimed under John B. Gamache, senior, by his legal representatives.

8. The certified extract from the minutes of Recorder Hunt, taken under the act of Congress of 26th of May, 1824, [is] evidence that the tract of land therein mentioned and described was claimed and inhabited, cultivated or possessed, by John B. Gamache, senior, prior to the 20th day of December, 1803, and evidence that the same was confirmed to John B. Gamache, senior, or his legal representatives, by the act of Congress of 13th June, 1812.

9. The certified extract from [the] registry of certificates from the recorder's office, offered in evidence [by the plaintiffs, is evidence] that the out lot therein mentioned was confirmed to John B. Gamache, senior, or his legal representatives, by the act of 13th June, 1812.

10. The certified extract from the list of claims transmitted by the recorder of land titles to the surveyor-general, and certified from the office of the surveyor-general, relating to the claims of the legal representatives of John B. Gamache, senior, is evidence of said claim and the extent and boundary thereof, and that the same was confirmed by the act of Congress of 13th June, 1812.

11. The certificate of confirmation of the recorder of land titles in Missouri, given in evidence by the plaintiffs, shows a prim a facie title from the United States, in the legal representatives of John B. Gamache, senior, to the land therein described,

To which decision of the court, refusing said instructions, the plaintiffs by their counsel excepted.

Page 57 U.S. 451, 457

The defendants then asked the following instructions, which were given by the court, as follows, to wit:

Instructions given to defendants. 5. If the jury find that the land spoken of by the witnesses as actually cultivated and possessed by Gamache did not embrace the land now in dispute, they ought to find for the defendants.

17. The survey No. 120, read by the plaintiffs, is no evidence of title, nor of the extent and boundaries of Gamache's claim.

18. The testimony taken before Hunt, and read in evidence by the plaintiff, is not to be regarded by the jury in the present case, the defendant insisting that the claim had been abandoned.

To the giving of which instructions the [plaintiffs] by their counsel excepted.

The verdict being for the defendants, the case was carried by the plaintiffs to the Supreme Court of Missouri, where the judgment of the court below was affirmed. It was then brought to this court by the plaintiffs, by a writ of error, issued under the twenty-fifth section of the Judiciary Act.

It was argued by Mr. Holmes, for the plaintiffs in error, and Mr. Picot, for the defendants. Only those points will be noted which are connected with the decision of the court. The counsel for the plaintiffs in error made the following: III. The certificate of the recorder of land titles, offered in evidence in this case, dated the 22d of January, 1839, was competent and admissible evidence of the facts necessary to give title under and by virtue of the act of 13th June, 1812, and showed a prim a facie title in the legal representatives of Gamache, of the date of that act, to the lot therein described. Macklot v. Dubreuil, 9 Mo. 489, a certificate issued in

1842 held good, and evidence of title; Boyce v. Papin, 11 Mo. 16; Hunter v. Hemphill, 6 Mo. 106; and Sarpy v. Papin, 7 Mo. 503, one in possession, merely, not showing a title, cannot question the certificate, or survey; Soulard v. Allen, (Sup. Court of Mo., Oct. term, 1853,) a certificate issued by Conway, since 1839, held good. The objection of the Supreme Court of Missouri to this case of Camache v. Piquignot is based on the omission of this claim in the first list sent to the surveyor-general. No limit of time was fixed by the terms, or spirit of the act, within which the certificate must be issued, after proof made within the eighteen months prescribed, or when the power of the recorder to issue it was to cease.

IV. The certified extract from the registry of certificates was competent evidence, that the certificate, authorized by the act

Page 57 U.S. 451, 458

of 26th May, 1824, had been duly issued by the recorder of land titles, for the claim therein mentioned and described, and that the same had been confirmed by the act of 13th June, 1812. McGill v. Somers, 15 Mo. 80; Biehler v. Coonce, 9 Mo. 351, an extract from this same registry of certificates held admissible evidence; Roussin v. Parks, 8 Mo. 544.

V. The certified extract from the surveyor-general's list of claims proved was competent evidence that this claim had been officially reported to him by the recorder of land titles, as a claim that had been duly proved before him within the eighteen months, and that the surveyor- general had authority by law to survey it, as such. McGill v. Somers, and other cases cited: the act of Congress of the 29th April, 1816, 3 Stat. at Large, 324, authorized the survey to be made.

VI. The certified extract from the books of Hunt's minutes of testimony, was competent and admissible evidence, for the purpose of showing, that whatever title the government had in this the government and the claimants had passed to the claimants; a matter in which the defendants, as third persons, had no interest and no concern, at least until they should show some prior or superior title to this land. McGill v. Somers, 15 Mo. R. 80-86, extracts from these same 'recorder's (Hunt's) minutes,' and from the surveyor-general's list, held admissible evidence as good as the certificate itself. Biehler v. Coonce, 9 Mo. 351; Roussin v. Parks, 8 Mo. 544.

1. On the same principle as a deed that constitutes a link in a plaintiff's chain of title, and to which the defendant may be no party nor privy; and

2. On the principle of a deposition taken to perpetuate testimony, the government and the claimants being the only parties concerned in the effect of it, and both being present at the taking of it, by authority of the act of Congress.

3. Like a deposition, it is evidence tending to prove the existence of the facts prior to 1803, necessary to bring this out lot within the operation of the act of 1812, as a grant of title.

4. The Supreme Court of Missouri, (Gamble, J., delivering the opinion of the court in this case,) affected to treat this testimony of witnesses as if it had been some mere volunteer 'affidavits' of the parties themselves, made extrajudicially, and without authority of law. In McGill v. Somers, the same judge (delivering the opinion of the court) held an extract from these same 'minutes,' to be evidence as good as the certificate. In Soulard v. Allen, October them, 1853, Scott, J., delivering the opinion of the court, (Gamble, J., not sitting,) held a certificate of Conway (recorder) issued upon these 'minutes' of testimony to be good evidence.

Page 57 U.S. 451, 459

All the certificates that have been issued by Hunt or Conway, since the eighteen months expired, were necessarily based on these 'minutes' of the proof made. Memory of three large volumes of proof was out of the question; and the surveyor-generals list was not a record of the recorder's office, otherwise than as Hunt's books of minutes were the original from which that list was drawn off as an abstract, in 1827.

5. Nothing had been done by any officer of the government at the date of the taking of this testimony, in relation to the claim of commons, that recognized any right or title of the inhabitants of the town of Carondelet to the land included in this outlet as commons.

The survey of the commons, No. 3102, and the outline survey of the common field, No. 3103, were made in 1834.

VII. The fact that this claim had been omitted in the first list furnished by recorder Hunt to the surveyor-general, and that it was not reported till the 12th of March, 1839, has no legal effect whatever on the title or any right of the claimant under the act of the 26th of May, 1824, nor upon the validity or admissibility of the above documents as evidence; for,

1. The entry of the claim in the books of Hunt's minutes as a claim proved and the certificate issued upon it, as such, are the proper legal evidence of the decision of the recorder of land titles upon the sufficiency of the proof made. Macklot v. Dubreuil, 9 Mo. 490: the recorder passed upon the facts referred to him when he issued the certificate; the point was made in Mr. Gamble's brief, that the recorder had no authority to issue a certificate in 1842, but it was not specially noticed in the opinion of the court, which held the certificate good.

2. The powers conferred and the duties imposed by the act were conferred and imposed on the recorder of land titles, (a perpetual officer,) and not upon Theodore Hunt, merely; he was expressly required, by the third section of the act, to issue such a certificate, and no limit of time was fixed by the act within which he was to make his decision on the proof taken within the eighteen months, or report the claims to the surveyor, or issue the certificate, nor in which his power to do so was to cease, otherwise than by a complete performance of the duties imposed on him. Act of the 26th of May, 1824, 4 Stat. at Large, 65.

3. The second clause of the third section of that act, requiring a list of claims proved to be furnished the surveyor-general, was merely directory, and imposed a ministerial duty only on the recorder of

land titles, touching the internal administration of the land-office, and it was not intended by the act to be a condition precedent to the issuing of a certificate, nor even

Page 57 U.S. 451, 460

to the right of the claimant to have a survey made of his claim, according to law, as a confirmed lot. Lytle v. State of Arkansas, 9 How. 314-333. Perry v. O'Hanlon, 11 Mo. 589-595: parties are not to be prejudiced by delays and omissions of merely ministerial officers and government agents. Taylor v. Brown, 5 Cranch, 234: a law requiring an officer to record surveys within two months, and return a list, is merely directory, and the validity of the survey is not affected, if not done. In point by principle and analogy.

4. The certificate containing an accurate description of the lot, so that any surveyor could find it, was all the evidence of title the claimants needed; and no public survey was necessary for them, though a convenience to them, as well as to the government.

Ott v. Soulard, 9 Mo. 603-4, where the calls are ascertained by the grant, the construction is then matter of law for the court. Menard's Heirs v. Massey, 8 How. 293, as to certainty of description, 'Id certum est,' &c. Smith v. U. States, 10 Pet. 338: a grant is good if capable of definite location by its description, without a survey. Chouteau v. Eckhart, 2 How. 344: an act gives title, if the land can be identified as confirmed without resort to a survey. United States v. Lawton, 5 How. 10: the identity of the land granted may be established by the face of the grant, or by survey.

The proof made ascertains, (for the certificate,) designates, and proves the tract, which was granted by the act of 1812.

5. The list of claims proved was not required to be sent to the surveyor-general for the purpose of being the only and conclusive evidence for or against the claimants, nor was it made so by the terms or nature of the act, either of the fact that a claim had been proved and a certificate issued, or of the recorder's decision on the proof; nor was it of any importance to the claimant whether the claims were all reported at once or not; but the first list was sufficient information and good evidence for the surveyor-general of what it contained, and the supplementary lists were likewise good evidence, and sufficient to authorize a survey to be made of the claims reported, when reported.

6. No limit of time was fixed within which, if claims proved were not reported, they should never be reported at all. One object of the act was to get information for the surveyor-general, and obviously, the sooner he got it, and the whole of it, the better.

7. When the first list had been furnished to the surveyor-general, nearly two years after the expiration of the 18 months prescribed for the taking of the proof, (then supposed by the

Page 57 U.S. 451, 461

recorder to contain all,) and when, by supplementary lists, the omissions had been supplied, and the errors corrected, the act of Congress had then only, and not before, been fully and substantially complied with, in this repect.

8. Any merely extra-legal inference to be drawn from the fact of the omission is rebutted by the fact, that there were other omissions and errors, certified by Hunt himself to have been errors in transcribing the former list from the books in his office, (Hunt's minutes,) and conclusively rebutted, by the fact that a certificate was issued; for if the recorder's opinion had been against the claim, at first, the issuing of a certificate shows that he had changed that opinion, and was satisfied with the proof.

9. The omission and delay have prejudiced nobody. The lot has not been set apart for schools, as a vacant lot, nor would it have been included in the survey of the commons, by Brown, if the commons belonging to the village had been surveyed according to their claim and confirmation, as directed by the 2d section of the act of 26th May, 1824, nor if he had consulted the records of the recorder's office, and the proof there made of this claim, as he ought to have done.

This out lot was surveyed by Brown, at the same time, and under the same instructions, as the other town lots, out lots, and common fields of Carondelet, (in 1839.) Brown might as well have included other common fields as this one in his survey of commons, in 1834. Many of them were never proved before the recorder.

The counsel for the defendant in error made (amongst others) the following points:--

I. The list returned by recorder Hunt, (certified to include a description of all the lots proved up before him,) which does not include a description of the Gamache claim, is conclusive against the plaintiffs. 3d sec. act of May 26, 1824, Statutes at Large, vol. 4, p. 66.

1. Whether, if the plaintiffs had a certificate of confirmation issued by Hunt for their claim, they could dispute the correctness of the list need not be inquired into, seeing that the plaintiffs have no such certificate.

The statute, however, designated two distinct matters of evidence which it would seem were both required to be possessed by a party claiming the benefits of the law. First, the certificate. This was intrusted to the claimant, whose claim was confirmed, and the plaintiffs should either have produced the certificate, or at least shown that it was issued. Second, the list. This was retained by the government as the record of what was confirmed; and the plaintiffs should have shown

Page 57 U.S. 451, 462

that it included their claim. In this case it appears, affirmatively, that no such certificate was ever issued, and that neither the list nor the copy thereof embraces this claim.

2. It is not necessary, for the disposal of this case, to inquire into the validity of the acts of recorder Hunt in making supplemental and explanatory returns to the surveyor, subsequent to his return of the list required by law, seeing that the plaintiffs' claim is not included in any such return. Whether such acts were valid or not, they are cumulative evidence against the claim of plaintiffs. They go to show, that even after reviewing and revising his decisions, the recorder persevered in his rejection of the claim of Gamache's representatives.

3. The recorder expressly certified that the list contains all the lots confirmed by him. Courts cannot look behind that list. Similar lists have always been considered as binding on the ministerial departments of the government.

4. In the list are included numerous claims, proved before, and certified by the recorder as confirmed, and which were embraced within the limits of the claim. He must necessarily have decided against the Gamache claim in deciding in favor of the adversary claims.

The recorder acted in a judicial capacity in the execution of the extraordinary duties imposed on him by the act of 1824, and his decisions are res adjudicatae.

II. The certificate of confirmation issued by recorder Conway in 1839, is merely void. 1. It is void on its face. 2. It is void for want of jurisdiction. The general powers of the recorder, as denoted by his title, are purely clerical, and are set forth in the law creating the office. See sections 3 and 4 of act of March 2, 1805, Statutes at Large, vol. 2, p. 326. The powers given to the recorder by the act of 1824, were extraordinary and judicial. Upon their execution the office as to such extraordinary powers became functus officio. The powers, if not exhausted, ceased by limitation. First, eighteen months from the passage of the act, the power to receive claims and evidence, expressly ended by the terms of the first section.

The second section, although confined to regulating the duties of the surveyor, looks to a prompt determination of the duties of the recorder. How could the surveyor, immediately after the expiration of the eighteen months, designate the vacant lots, (namely those not certified and listed by the recorder as confirmed) unless the recorder had previously performed those duties? The third section contemplates the issuing of the recorder's certificates within the eighteen months. After providing for

Page 57 U.S. 451, 463

them, it proceeds to require, further, that so soon as the said term shall have expired, the recorder shall furnish the surveyor with a list of the lots so proved. The list was designed to embrace the certified lots only. The act contemplates the impossibility of the recorder preserving in his breast during a term of near eighteen months, the remembrance of many hundreds of decisions, and points out the certificates, or registry thereof, as the record which he shall preserve of the lots 'so proved,' and from which he is to compile his list. The making and transmitting the list was the final act. That done, the powers conferred by the law ceased.

Secondly. Although the office and general powers of the recorder are perpetual, yet special and temporary powers given for a particular purpose, will not endure forever.

Granting that the powers conferred by the act of 1824, were not simply conferred on Hunt, the recorder for the time being, but on his office; yet to have authorized Conway, or any successor, to have issued a certificate of confirmation, such successor should have succeeded to the office during the prescribed term of eighteen months, and the proof must have been made before him.

3. The head of the land department on the appeal of the plaintiffs, has decided that the proceedings of Conway were of no avail under the law.

III. The abstract from the registry of confirmations issued by Conway, is void. The certificate itself being a 'mere nullity' as declared by the Supreme Court of Missouri, the fact that it was issued, and when, is of no importance. Its only use in the case is to show affirmatively, what might otherwise appear only negatively, that recorder Hunt issued no certificate of confirmation.

IV. The extracts from Hunt's minutes are not evidence. 1. Hunt was not a commissioner to take testimony, and the affidavits were received without notice, the co-defendant in this suit being then in the actual possession of the land.

2. The act required no recorded or written proof before the recorder, and the circumstance that affidavits were taken by Hunt, touching the Gamache claim, is no evidence that he considered it as proved to have been inhabited, cultivated or possessed, prior to the 20th December, 1803, and that the land claimed was an out lot. 3. On the contrary, the circumstance that the claim was not entered in his list, is decisive to show that he was not satisfied with the proof. V. The return of the description of the Gamache claim to the surveyor, by Conway, in 1839, was merely null, and afforded no evidence of title whatever.

Page 57 U.S. 451, 464

The abuses to which such a practice will lead are manifest. If Hunt's list may be altered after twelve years have elapsed, alterations may be made at any distance of time; if future recorders may supply fancied omissions, they may strike out such claims as they may regard as erroneously entered; if they can thus deal with the list of Hunt, they can do the same with Bates's confirmations, and the numerous land titles depending on the action of the recorders of former days, will lie at the mercy of officers, selected not for their capacity to judge of the proofs of titles, but for their fidelity in taking care of books and papers.

Mr. Justice CATRON delivered the opinion of the court.

This case was brought here by writ of error to the Supreme Court of Missouri, and presents questions alleged to be cognizable in this court under the 25th section of the Judiciary Act. The plaintiffs claimed a tract of land of six arpents in front, and forty back, lying adjoining to the village of Carondelet, in Missouri. It was claimed as 'an out lot' which had been confirmed by the act of Congress of June 13th, 1812, to John B. Gamache, the ancestor of the plaintiffs.

In support of this position there was offered, in evidence, certain documents issued from the office of the recorder of land titles. The first was a paper claimed to be a certificate of confirmation issued by Conway, the recorder of land titles, dated 22d January, 1839, under the act of Congress of the 26th May, 1824. The second was an extract from the registry kept by the recorder of certificates, issued by him under the act of 1824, by which it appears that Conway entered the certificate of Gamache's representatives on that register on the 12th March, 1839, and furnished on that day to the surveyor-general a description of the land. The third was an extract from the additional list of claims furnished by the recorder to the surveyor-general on the 12th March, 1839, which addition was of the Gamache claim alone. There were other documents showing that Hunt, who was the recorder of land titles, who acted under the act of 1824 in taking proof of claims, and who filed with the surveyor the list of claims proved before him, had filed one or two supplemental or explanatory lists after the first.

The court below rejected the evidence offered.

A survey of the claim of Gamache was made by a deputy surveyor under instructions from the surveyor-general, and the survey being returned to the office by the deputy and a plat made, the word 'approved' was written upon it and signed by the then surveyor-general, but it never was recorded. It appeared, in evidence, that the practice of the surveyor's office,

Page 57 U.S. 451, 465

when a deputy surveyor made return of a survey which he had been instructed to make, was, to have the survey examined, to see the manner in which the deputy had followed the instructions given, and if he had followed them, his work was approved, and the approval evidenced by such writing as had been made in this case, which was intended to authorize the payment of the deputy for his work; and that subsequently the survey was more carefully examined, and if found to be a proper survey in all respects it was recorded in the books of the office, which was the evidence that it was finally adopted and approved, and that by the practice of the office certified copies of surveys were not given out until they were thus finally approved and recorded. Conway, who had been surveyor-general as well as recorder, testified that he would regard the survey of the Gamache claim as an approved survey, and would record it as such if he were in the office.

It appeared, in evidence, that the present surveyor-general refused to record it as an approved survey, or to certify it to the recorder as a survey of land for which a certificate of confirmation is to issue, and that in that refusal he is sustained by the department at Washington.

After the evidence was closed, the court, by an instruction, declared that the survey was not evidence of title, nor of the boundaries and extent of Gamache's claim.

A certified copy of the affidavits made before recorder Hunt, when he was taking proof under the act of 1824, was in evidence, but an instruction given to the jury substantially excluded them from consideration.

On this state of facts the Supreme Court of Missouri held, among other things, as follows:

> 'In the present case we have a recorder of land titles, fourteen years from the passage of this act, attempting to give the evidence of title, by issuing a certificate of confirmation, and certifying the claim to the surveyor-general as one confirmed by the act of 1812. If the government of the United States has confirmed the title set up by the plaintiffs by that act of Congress, then the party, as has been held in this court, does not lose his land by the failure to procure the evidence provided for by the act of 1824; and under these decisions the plaintiffs in this case, after the evidence was rejected, which they claimed was rightly issued under the last-mentioned act, proceeded to prove the cultivation and possession of their ancestor, Gamache, and claimed that the title was confirmed by the act of 1812.'
> 'If the evidence of title, purporting to be issued under the act of 1824, appeared undisputed by the United States, and

acknowledged and treated by the government as effectual, then it may

Page 57 U.S. 451, 466

be that a person who was a mere stranger to the title would not be allowed to dispute the correctness of the conduct of the officers in their attempt to carry out the law. But when we find that the government itself, in its own officers, arrests the progress of the title, and the whole reliance of the party in this case is upon the acts of the recorder, the correctness of which is denied by the government, we will examine his acts and give them effect only so far as they conform to the law.'

'That the recorder, under the act of 1824, was required to act in a quasi judicial character, is perfectly manifest, although there was no mode provided by the law for the expression of an opinion against the sufficiency of the evidence given before him. If a claim was, in his judgment, confirmed by the act of 1812, he issued to the party a certificate of confirmation, and included the lot in the descriptive list which he was required to furnish the surveyor-general. If there was a failure to prove the inhabitation, cultivation, or possession to his satisfaction, he simply omitted to include the claim in his list, and he issued no certificate.'

'The acts required to be done when a claim was confirmed, were to be done immediately after the expiration of the time limited for taking the proof; and when we see, from the evidence offered by the plaintiff, that the recorder filed his list of confirmations with the surveyor in October, 1827, near twelve years before Conway, his successor, returned the present claim to that office, we cannot avoid the conclusion that this latter act was not within the scope allowed for such proceeding by the act of Congress. It is not necessary to maintain that if Hunt, the recorder who took the proof, had died before he acted upon the claims, his successor could not act upon them; but when he did act, and made out and furnished to the surveyor the list required by law, the conclusion is one which the law draws, that claims not within that list are claims not proved to his satisfaction.'

The claim of Gamache was anxiously prosecuted before the department of public lands at Washington during the pendency of this suit, and was there decided by the commissioner in conformity to the decision of the Supreme Court of Missouri; and which decision was confirmed by the Secretary of the Interior in September last. The reasons for this decision are here given in the language of the commissioner in reply to the plaintiffs' counsel, prosecuting the claim.

'The surveyor-general at St. Louis having declined to approve the survey as made by Brown for Gamache, and to certify the same to the recorder-You apply to this office to give orders to surveyor-general Clark, 'requiring him to return the

Page 57 U.S. 451, 467

survey of the tract of six by forty arpens in the name of John B. Gamache, sr., or his legal representatives, to the recorder of land titles, and that the recorder be directed to issue to 'you' a certificate of confirmation in the usual form, that 'you' may have the evidence of your title in the usual form for the purpose of prosecuting your rights in the courts having competent jurisdiction.'

'In behalf of the representatives of Gamache it is maintained that they are confirmed by the act of 13th June, 1812.
'The first section of the supplemental act of 26th of May, 1824, made it the duty of the individual owners or claimants whose lots were confirmed by the act of 1812 on the ground of inhabitation, cultivation, or possession prior to the 20th of December, 1803, 'to proceed within eighteen months after the passage of the act of 1824,' to designate their said lots by proving before the recorder of land titles for said State and territory the fact of such inhabitation, cultivation, or possession, and the boundaries and extent of each claim, so

as to enable the surveyor- general to distinguish the private from the vacant lots appertaining to the said towns and villages.'

'The third section of the said act of 1824 made it the duty of the recorder to issue a certificate of confirmation for each claim confirmed, but further declares as follows:

'And so soon as the said term shall have expired, he shall furnish the surveyor-general with a list of the lost so proved to have been inhabited, cultivated, or possessed, to serve as his guide in distinguishing them from the vacant lots to be set apart as above described, and shall transmit a copy of such list to the commissioner of the general land-office.'

'A report or list, purporting to contain all the claims proved up under the said act of 1824, was accordingly returned to this office in 1827, but that list does not embrace this particular claim of Gamache for 6 x 40 arpens within the limits of the Carondelet Commons.

We have no power to look behind that list in order to determine what has or has not been confirmed any more than we could look behind the face of a report of a board of commissioners or of the recorder, which had been confirmed by a law of Congress, and take cognizance of a case not embraced by such report, even if satisfied that it had been omitted by the reporting officer through inadvertence. This is a well-settled principle. See instructions to register and receiver, 13th April, 1835. 2d part Birchard's Comp. printed laws, instructions and opinions, page 757, &c.

'As the 3d section of the act of 26th of May, 1824, then expressly declares that the list to be furnished by the recorder

'shall serve as a guide' to the surveyor-general in the execution of the duties devolved on him by the act, and as it is not shown that the claim in question is embraced by that list, neither that officer, nor this office, has the power to treat the claim in question as confirmed and entitled to an approved survey, and, consequently, in my opinion, the

> commissioner has not the legal ability to comply with your application in the premises.'

With the correctness of these decisions of the Supreme Court of Missouri and the department of public lands we entirely concur. Nor will we add any views of our own in support of the State decision, for the reason that the questions here presented are peculiarly local, being limited to the city of St. Louis and a few villages in the State of Missouri, the public at large having no concern with any question presented in this cause. And after due consideration we here take occasion to say, that although it is in the power of this court, and made its duty, to review all cases coming here from State courts of last resort, in which was drawn in question and construed prejudicial to a party's claim, the Constitution, or a law of the United States, or an authority exercised under them, still, in this peculiarly local class of cases asserting titles to town and village lots, confirmed by the act of 1812, we feel exceedingly indisposed to disturb the State decisions. So far the ability and soundness they manifest have commanded our entire concurrence and respect, and are likely to do so in future. It is proper further to remark that the jury was instructed, at the request of the plaintiffs, that inhabitation and cultivation of a part of the lot, claiming the whole, would be good for the whole within the meaning of the act of 1812.

The jury was also instructed, at the defendant's request, 'that if the land spoken of by the witnesses as actually cultivated and possessed by Gamache, did not embrace the land now in dispute, they ought to find for the defendants.'

In regard to these instructions the State court held that:

> 'The first instruction given for the defendant, if it stood alone, would be so entirely erroneous as to require a reversal of the judgment. That the jury should be required to find for the defendant, if the cultivation by the elder Gamache was not a cultivation of the precise piece of ground in controversy, would have been so gross a mistake, that neither the court nor the counsel asking the instruction could be supposed to have fallen into it. Accordingly, when we

examine the second instruction given for the plaintiff, we find the court telling the jury that the cultivation of a part of a tract, under claim of the whole, was, under the act of 1812, a cultivation of the whole tract;

Page 57 U.S. 451, 469

and, in looking into the case, we see that the controversy was whether this cultivation of Gamache was not on an entirely different tract from that now claimed to include the premises in dispute. 'We are satisfied that the jury must have understood the question to be, whether the cultivation of Gamache, spoken of by the witnesses, was at any place upon the tract to which his heirs now claim title, or at some place upon an entirely different tract. In this view of the question submitted to the jury, there would be no propriety in reversing the judgment for the instruction given for the defendant.'

The instructions asked by the plaintiffs, which were refused by the court, all refer to the proceedings in the recorder's office, the effect of which has been considered. On the whole it is ordered that the judgment be affirmed.

Order.

This cause came on to be heard, on the transcript of the record, from the Supreme Court of the State of Missouri, and was argued by counsel. On consideration whereof, it is now here ordered and adjudged by this court, that the judgment of the said Supreme Court, in this cause, be, and the same is hereby affirmed, with costs.

Printed in the United States
120785LV00002B/1/P